Other Books by Peter Stansky

AMBITIONS AND STRATEGIES: THE STRUGGLE FOR THE LEADERSHIP
OF THE LIBERAL PARTY IN THE 1890's

ENGLAND SINCE 1867

With William Abrahams

JOURNEY TO THE FRONTIER: TWO ROADS TO THE SPANISH
CIVIL WAR

THE UNKNOWN ORWELL

Edited by Peter Stansky

THE LEFT AND WAR: THE BRITISH LABOUR PARTY AND
WORLD WAR I

JOHN MORLEY: NINETEENTH-CENTURY ESSAYS

CHURCHILL: A PROFILE

THE VICTORIAN REVOLUTION

The Library of World Biography

Gladstone

A Progress in Politics

By Peter Stansky

THE LIBRARY OF WORLD BIOGRAPHY
J. H. PLUMB, GENERAL EDITOR

Little, Brown and Company — Boston – Toronto

FIRST EDITION

Library of Congress Cataloging in Publication Data

Stansky, Peter.
  Gladstone, a progress in politics.

  (The Library of world biography)
  Bibliography: p.
  Includes index.
  1. Gladstone, William Ewart, 1809–1898.
  2. Great Britain—Politics and government—1837–1901.
  3. Prime ministers—Great Britain—Biography.
  I. Title.
  DA563.4.S73 1979   941.081′092′4 [B]   79–586
  ISBN 0-316-81058-4

BP

*Published simultaneously in Canada
by Little, Brown & Company (Canada) Limited*

PRINTED IN THE UNITED STATES OF AMERICA

For Stan

Contents

Foreword

THE VICTORIAN AGE IN BRITAIN was dominated by two statesmen—Benjamin Disraeli* and William Ewart Gladstone—who stamped their personalities on the imaginations, hopes and fears of their fellow countrymen more extensively than any previous Englishmen save military heroes like Nelson and Wellington. Surely, Pitt had been the idol of the city of London, and John Wilkes had been widely known throughout the provinces as well as in London, but neither were known to millions of workingmen and women as were "Dizzy" and the "Grand Old Man." And the commitment to Gladstone was wider and deeper than to Disraeli. Thousands of men and women named a male child after him: in some families the naming has gone on for generations.

Gladstone brought moral force to politics. Indeed, his career was a long political pilgrimage, plagued at times by agonizing doubt and frequently plunged into crisis by moral conviction. Gladstone began life as a committed high Tory Anglican and ended as the epitome of liberalism and the darling of nonconformists. Disraeli might be regarded, even applauded, for his acrobatic feats of expediency, but every change, every political maneuver even, of Gladstone's, seemed to be clothed in a deep sense of truth, sincerity and honest purpose. Rarely in the his-

* See R. W. Davis, *Disraeli*. Library of World Biography.

tory of mankind has so strong a moral attitude been linked with practical politics. This in itself would make Gladstone a figure of outstanding importance but his career and personality add further fascinating and complex dimensions to his stature.

He was highly intellectual—possibly the best read statesman of modern times, versed in the classics, in medieval and modern theology, and a master of his country's literary culture. In addition he was an excellent mathematician and knowledgeable about the sciences. He was deeply and genuinely, indeed almost painfully, religious and at the same time powerfully and, to himself, distressingly sensual, a conflict that drove him to self-flagellation on the one hand and to the pursuit of whores in the street on the other. Not, however, for relief but in the hope of converting them, an activity dreaded by his colleagues and singular in a Prime Minister. His personality, brilliantly analyzed by Peter Stansky, was one of great force and complexity: he was, in every way, larger than life, and from his youth onwards, he had the air of immortality.

His political odyssey was in keeping with his personality: a somewhat slow progression towards the political center, then a somewhat more rapid move to its left; a demonstration of exceptional administrative skill and integrity when in office, which, of course, he achieved young; a gradually developing sense that Providence had made him the conscience of his fellow countrymen, their voice in protest against injustice and inhumanity. He was capable—as in the Midlothian campaign—of holding audiences enthralled with a highly complex rhetoric. In a sense he achieved the success of a demagogue without being in any way like one. He could, of course, disenchant and infuriate, not just Queen Victoria, but large elements, and powerful ones, in his nation. His failure to support Gordon adequately at Khartoum and his conversion to Home Rule for Ireland were but dramatic highlights of a career that often teetered on the edge of failure. But the prospect of defeat, of a career in ruins, could never deter Gladstone from what he felt to be not only the right moral course but also the right political action. And his political instincts were better, more percipient, alas, than those of the majority of his country or party. The wanton extension of imperial domination was inherently dangerous for Britain, as Gladstone realized and as the history of the twentieth century has shown. The history of Ireland has clearly demonstrated how right—strategically—Gladstone was in his approach to the Irish problem.

Gladstone remains the colossus of modern English politics, approached only in stature by Lloyd George and Winston Churchill, and a worthy subject therefore for biography. He has never been better served than in this short life by Peter Stansky. In a most original and effective way, Stansky shows Gladstone's strengths and weaknesses, both by skillful interpretation and by a most effective and cunning use of Gladstone's own words.

—J. H. Plumb

Preface

ONE QUITE PROPERLY FEELS HESITANT to offer yet
another life of William Ewart Gladstone, brief as this
one is. Many have been written; many more will be. In
any case, no final biography—if there can ever be such a
creature—can appear until Colin Matthew finishes his
exemplary editing of the Gladstone diaries. And since it
is hard to imagine that any other scholar will then know
Gladstone so well, it is good news that Mr. Matthew himself will write such a life. It should be a worthy successor
to the biography published in 1903 by John Morley, a
biography flawed in some ways, particularly in its failure
to pay sufficient attention to the importance of Gladstone's religiosity to his life. Perhaps Philip Magnus's
valuable biography of 1954 went a little too far in the
other direction, overemphasizing Gladstone's role as a
religious exemplar, but not giving him sufficient credit
as a practical politician. Both these biographers had a
wide range of primary material at their disposal, and that
material has now increased with the availability of many
more family papers to be found in the Record Office at
Hawarden, a resource exploited by Joyce Marlowe in
The Oak and the Ivy (1977). Useful brief lives are
Gladstone and Liberalism (1952), the excellent study begun by the distinguished historian and Gladstone scholar
J. L. Hammond and finished by M. R. D. Foot, and most
recently *Gladstone* (1975) by E. J. Feuchtwanger.

Why, then, would one have the temerity to offer yet another brief life? The work of biography is never done —and one hopes that differing approaches to one subject continue to have some value. Also I have attempted something different in this particular study—not, as far as I know, available elsewhere: to approach Gladstone through a discussion of some of his great parliamentary speeches, and at the same time to provide a short biographical essay—I trust not too selective a one.

Allow me to thank William Abrahams, A. F. Thompson, Jean Whitnack, Nancy Ray and Loraine Sinclair. And I would like to thank Larned Bradford and J. H. Plumb for their patience, as well as some graduate students at Stanford who were subjected to discussions of Gladstone more times than they may care to remember.

—Peter Stansky

A Gladstone Chronology

Prologue

1809   December 29. William Ewart Gladstone is born in Liverpool, the fourth and last son of John and Anne Gladstone.

1821   through 1827. He attends Eton.

1828   He enters Christ Church, Oxford.

1830   Elected President of the Oxford Union.

1831   December. He receives a "double first" in classics and mathematics.

1. Slavery

1832   Spring. The Reform Bill passes, extending the franchise and redistributing seats in the House of Commons.

December. Elected to Parliament as Member for Newark.

1833   March. Elected a member of the Tory Carlton Club (he remains a member until 1860).

June 3. He delivers his first major speech in Parliament: on slavery.

August. Abolition of slavery in the Colonies.

2. Religion

1834 December. Appointed Junior Lord of the Treasury in the first Administration of Sir Robert Peel.

1835 January. Appointed Undersecretary for War and the Colonies. He continues in the post until April, when the Government resigns.

July. Lord Melbourne becomes the Whig Prime Minister, remaining in the post through August 1841.

1837 June 20. King William IV dies; Victoria becomes Queen.

1838 His first book, *The State in Its Relations with the Church,* is published.

1839 July 25. He marries Catherine Glynne.

1840 He opposes the first Opium War in China, which had begun in November 1839.

1841 September. Appointed Vice-President of the Board of Trade and Master of the Mint in Peel's second Government. Under Peel's guidance, he is deeply involved in financial affairs (tariffs, customs) and speaks frequently in Parliament.

1843 May. Appointed President of the Board of Trade and enters the Cabinet.

1845 January 28. He resigns from the Cabinet.

February 4. Delivers the speech explaining his resignation.

3. Foreign Policy

1845 December. He is back in the Cabinet as Secretary of State for the Colonies.

1846 June. Peel's Government falls, having passed the repeal of the Corn Laws. Gladstone is out of office. He is also out of Parliament, having resigned, as was necessary, when he entered the Cabinet and not having put himself forward again in Newark, a protectionist constituency.

1847 August. General Election. He is elected a Member for Oxford University.

1848 Sworn in as a special constable in London to protect the city against possible Chartist riots.

1850 June 27. He delivers his speech on the Don Pacifico affair.

July 20. The death of Peel, Gladstone's most important political mentor.

October, to February 1851. He visits Naples.

1851 March 25. He delivers a speech defending religious liberty.

July. He publishes *Two Letters to Lord Aberdeen,* attacking the Kingdom of Naples.

December. His father dies.

4. Finance

1852 February 27. The Conservative Government of Lord Derby replaces the Whig Government of Lord John Russell. Benjamin Disraeli becomes Chancellor of the Exchequer and is leader of the Government in the House of Commons.

December 16. Delivers his speech opposing Disraeli's Budget.

December 17. The Conservative Government resigns after its Budget is defeated. Lord Aberdeen forms a coalition Government, in which Gladstone is Chancellor of the Exchequer.

1853 April 18. He delivers his first Budget speech.

October 4. Outbreak of the Crimean War.

1854 March 28. Britain and France declare war against Russia.

1855 January 20. The fall of Aberdeen's ministry over the conduct of the Crimean War. Lord Palmerston forms a ministry with Gladstone continuing at the Exchequer. After several weeks he gives up the post.

1857 February. Gladstone condemns the bombardment of Canton. Palmerston wins the General Election, which endorses his aggressive Chinese policy.

1858 February. Palmerston resigns and Lord Derby forms a Tory ministry. He invites Gladstone to join the Government, but Gladstone declines.

Gladstone publishes *Studies on Homer and the Homeric Age.*

July 23. Removal of disabilities on Jews so that they can sit in Parliament.

November. Gladstone undertakes a mission to the Ionian Islands.

1859 May. General Election. Palmerston forms a ministry with Gladstone as Chancellor of the Exchequer.

1860 January 23. The commercial treaty between England and France is signed.

February 10. Gladstone delivers his speech on the commercial treaty and the Budget.

March 30. He resigns from the Carlton Club; from now on he is a member of the Liberal party.

1864 April 28. England abandons its protectorate over the Ionian Islands.

5. Reform

1864 May 11. Gladstone delivers a speech on extending the franchise.

1865 October 18. Palmerston dies.

November. General Election. Gladstone is defeated at Oxford, but elected at South Lancashire. Lord John

Russell becomes Prime Minister and Gladstone remains Chancellor of the Exchequer.

1866   March. He introduces a Reform Bill.

April 27. His second speech on extending the franchise.

June. The Reform Bill is defeated. Lord Derby becomes Prime Minister and remains in the post until February 1868.

1867   August. The Tories introduce and pass the second Reform Bill.

1868   February–December. Disraeli is Prime Minister for the first time.

March 16. Gladstone speaks in favor of the disestablishment of the Irish Church.

November. General Election. Liberal victory. Gladstone forms his first ministry as Prime Minister. He is now M.P. for Greenwich.

6. Ireland: Religion

1869   March 1. Gladstone delivers his speech on the disestablishment of the Anglican Church in Ireland.

July 26. Parliament passes the Disestablishment Bill.

1870   July 19. The Franco-Prussian War begins.

August. The first Irish Land Bill and Forster's Education Bill are passed.

1872   The Ballot Act makes voting secret.

1874   January. Parliament is dissolved.

February. The Conservatives win the General Election and Disraeli becomes Prime Minister.

November. Gladstone publishes *The Vatican Decrees in Their Bearing on Civil Allegiance.*

1875   January 13. Gladstone resigns the leadership of the Liberal party.

7. Foreign Policy

1876   The massacres in Bulgaria.
       September 6. Gladstone publishes *The Bulgarian Horrors and the Question of the East.*
       December 12, through January 20, 1877. The Constantinople Conference is held.

1877   Gladstone conducts an active political campaign against the Government.
       April 24. The Russo-Turkish War breaks out.
       May 7. Gladstone delivers his speech against British imperialism.

1878   March 3. The Treaty of San Stefano ends the Russo-Turkish War.
       June–July. The Congress of Berlin is held.
       July 30. Gladstone speaks on the Treaty of Berlin.

1879   He conducts his campaign for the parliamentary seat of Midlothian in Scotland.
       November 25. His first Midlothian speech against Disraeli's foreign policy.

1880   February. The second series of speeches at Midlothian.
       March 8. General Election. The Tories are defeated.
       April 28. Gladstone begins his second ministry.

8. Religious Liberty

1881   The Irish Coercion and Land acts passed.

1882   July 11. The British bombard Alexandria and in effect take control of Egypt.

1883   April 26. Gladstone delivers his speech on religious liberty in connection with the Bradlaugh case.
       May 3. The Affirmation Bill is defeated.

1884   January 18. Gordon is sent out to oversee the evacuation of the Egyptian garrison in the Sudan.

August. Gladstone orders a relief expedition to rescue Gordon.

and 1885. The third Reform Bill is passed, increasing the electorate from 3 million to 5 million.

1885   January 26. The Mahdi takes Khartoum; Gordon is killed in its defense.

June 9. The Liberals are defeated on the Budget. Gladstone resigns.

November. General Election. Gladstone is reelected for Midlothian.

9. Ireland: Home Rule

1886   January. Resignation of the Tories. Gladstone forms his third ministry, dedicated to passing Home Rule for Ireland. Splits in the Liberal party over Ireland.

April 8. Gladstone delivers his speech on Home Rule.

June 7. The Home Rule Bill is defeated.

June–July. General Election. Victory for the Conservatives.

July. Gladstone resigns.

August. Lord Salisbury forms a Tory ministry.

10. The House of Lords

1890   November–December. Parnell named as corespondent in a divorce case; his leadership of the Irish party ends.

1891   October. The Newcastle program is adopted by the National Liberal Federation and advocates various reforms, including Home Rule.

1892   July. The Liberals win the General Election and Gladstone forms his fourth ministry.

1893   September 1. The House of Commons passes a Home Rule Bill, but the House of Lords rejects it a week later. The issue is not pursued.

1894   March 1. Gladstone delivers his last speech as Prime Minister: a denunciation of the House of Lords.
        March 3. He resigns as Prime Minister.

1895   July. General Election. The Liberals are defeated. Gladstone does not run for Parliament.

1896   September 24. He delivers his last important public address: on the massacre of the Armenians by the Turks.

1898   May 19. Gladstone dies at his country house at Hawarden.

Gladstone

A Progress in Politics

Prologue

FOUR TIMES PRIME MINISTER OF GREAT BRITAIN, William Ewart Gladstone emerges from his age, in a life that almost spans the nineteenth century (1809–1898), as a dominating force: the preeminent Victorian, a legend personified. And yet he did not share many of the qualities that go by the name of Victorian, no more than did the Queen herself. Legends to the contrary, it would seem that what is most characteristic of an age is seldom found at its most typical among its giants.

I should acknowledge at the outset of this study that the feeling of our own age is somewhat antipathetic to Gladstone. Churchill in his *History of the English-Speaking Peoples* observes that "what gradually made him the most controversial figure of the century was his gift of rousing moral indignation both in himself and in the electorate." Moral fervor in a political leader is something we may look askance at, in particular as it motivates and explains the development of his political ideas. Questions of sincerity and hypocrisy are bound to arise. Critics of Gladstone claim to recognize in him those traits of piety and self-righteousness that make the Victorians distasteful to us. Yet even his most hostile critics accept his prime importance in the history of nineteenth-century England, and at the present time, when increasing emphasis is being put by historians on detailed studies of special aspects of the century, he figures in many of them as a central character.

Gladstone himself left considerable material for study, the most basic, of course, being the immense collection of many of his manuscripts—250,000 of them—given in 1930 to the British Museum. But even this is not complete. Family papers—approximately 50,000 items—are at the Flintshire Record Office at Hawarden, where his descendants still live at the castle; his diary, not yet open to scholars, is being meticulously edited, and six volumes, covering the years 1825–1868, have been published to date; there are also the many letters by him in other collections of manuscripts, his own extensive writings, and the vast number of speeches he delivered in Parliament and to the electorate—the productions of a long and unceasingly industrious life. No matter that in his formal religious affiliation he was a member of the Church of England; he was endowed with the Calvinist conscience, and it manifested itself in forms of which Samuel Smiles, the apostle of self-help, would have approved. "How doth the busy bee improve each shining hour" might have been the leitmotif of his way of life. Even his favorite form of exercise, chopping down trees on the Hawarden estate, had the virtue of being useful. It would seem that in Gladstone's life every possible waking moment was to be dedicated to self-improvement. (And—as his diaries have revealed—to self-examination.) This was an aim that he shared with his brother-in-law Lord Lyttelton; after their double wedding to the Glynne sisters, both men astounded their wives by using spare moments during their respective honeymoons for the reading of Greek and Latin texts.

Gladstone's interests were many. He immersed himself

in Biblical and Homeric scholarship. He prepared an edition of the sermons of Bishop Butler, the eighteenth-century divine devoted to defending conscience over self-interest. He read widely in ancient and modern literatures. He maintained an extensive correspondence. His days were full of visits and consultations. He contributed innumerable articles on political and other matters to the serious journals. He took an active part in raising a large family, which eventually grew to include his nephews and nieces, the twelve motherless Lyttelton children; his bachelor brother-in-law Sir Stephen Glynne (whose ill-fated attempt to make a fortune in iron and steel manu-facturing involved Gladstone in years of work to save the Hawarden estate); his widowed brother-in-law Henry Glynne and his daughters; not to speak of the fatherless Talbot children, and the various orphans, old ladies, and a few rescued prostitutes whom the philanthropic and warmhearted Mrs. Gladstone installed in houses on the Hawarden estate. Mrs. Gladstone did her best to protect her husband's time and energy, but it is hardly to be wondered at that he finally built himself a private study, called the Temple of Peace, where he could arrange his books, prepare and rehearse his speeches, read without interruption, and write.

A crowded life—yet no matter how extensive were his scholarly, literary, social, domestic, and theological in-terests, his chief activities, from youth to old age, were political, and it is with some aspects of these that I will concentrate in this brief biography. My intention, work-ing within a small compass, is to trace the development of his political attitudes, ideas, and beliefs primarily as they are revealed in his speeches in Parliament. I believe these speeches to be Gladstone's most significant political statements, the prime force—granting the importance of certain of the speeches "out of doors" to the electorate—by which he influenced his fellow lawmakers, and so helped to direct the political and social currents of his time.

Rather surprisingly, given the breadth and seriousness of his intellectual interests, he was himself unaffected by many of the dominant philosophical ideas of the age. Profoundly religious, he was rarely burdened by the doubts that troubled certain of his contemporaries, and went through his extraordinary career more or less untouched by the doctrines and practices that shaped the Cobdens, the Mills, the Huxleys, those figures who are held to be typical of Victorian liberalism. And yet, more than they, he came to represent a significant number of nineteenth-century aspirations.

His ancestry was Scottish, in which respect he was a combination of two major strains, with a mother of Highland, and a father of Lowland, descent. His grandfather, Thomas Gladstones, had been a corn merchant in Leith, and became a very successful trader in various goods. Thomas's son John eliminated the *s* from his name, emigrated to Liverpool, started as a dealer in grain, and expanded his activities to include the owning of ships, and of plantations in the West Indies, with two thousand slaves. But, though the Gladstone family were slave owners, they were not slave traders, and the family fortune, contrary to what was sometimes thought, was not enhanced by the profits from the slave trade. John Gladstone had considerable, but mostly unrealized, political ambitions. A Tory, he had largely to content himself with fervent and valuable support for George Canning, one of the chief figures in the party, first as Foreign Secretary and later as Prime Minister. In 1822 John

Gladstone had hoped to join Canning in the House of Commons as the second Member for Liverpool, but his candidacy was rejected in favor of that of William Huskisson. Indeed, the one time that he was elected to Parliament—for Berwick-on-Tweed in 1825, winning by three votes—he was unseated on charges of corruption. Thereafter he concentrated his political hopes on his sons—and it was clear fairly early that William was to be the most important standard-bearer for the family.

The traditional clash of temperament within Scotland between the sober, hardworking Lowlander and the fiery, impetuous Highlander seems to have been reflected in William Gladstone's opposing characteristics. John Morley describes his "union of impulse with caution, of passion with circumspection, of pride and fire with a steady foothold on the solid earth" and goes on to say that "we may perhaps find a sort of explanation in thinking of him as a highlander in the custody of a lowlander."[1]

What too often is taken for the "natural" phlegmatic temperament of the Englishman is instead frequently the result of a rigid self-control exercised over passionately held beliefs. This was certainly true of Gladstone—one generation removed from Scotland—who, however strongly he might feel, attempted to present his ideas with circumspection and logical argumentation in order to make them politically acceptable. And yet it was often the sense of an underlying, passionate conviction, a moral fervor not to be denied, that counted for more than lucid argumentation, and evoked from his listeners their enthusiastic response, most evident in the Midlothian campaigns of 1879 and 1880.

He owed his passionate nature to his mother, and it

was she also who shaped his religious life, raising him as an Evangelical within the Church of England. Gladstone was far from being the unimaginative bourgeois, the stolid, archetypal Victorian; rather, he was one of the last products of the Romantic era, full of passions and impossible ideals, determined to force himself *and his society* to go beyond their ordinary limitations and achieve a new and better world. His romanticism and Evangelicalism led him to believe that man could be transformed by his own efforts: it followed therefore that the effort should be made. He extended this belief to everyone who came within his ken: to his closest friends (for whom he entertained the highest expectations, an idealism as unwavering as his own, and so found their backslidings all the more painful) ; to the men and women of his own country; to the Italians, the Balkan Christians, and the Greeks; to all those who hoped, by their own efforts, to change and improve their situation.

At the same time that Gladstone possessed this romantic and missionary strain, he was also intensely practical and down-to-earth, like his father, John Gladstone, the Lowland Scot, that very successful, hardheaded Liverpool businessman, with his extensive interests in India and in the West Indies. The influence of the father upon the son is not to be underestimated; it was as potent in its way as that of the mother. A strong-willed man, he would not hesitate to interfere in his son's life, and did so most notably in 1830, when he dissuaded him from becoming a clergyman.

There were six children in the family. Of these, it was only the fifth, the extraordinary William, born in 1809, who truly distinguished himself—not his rather sour older brothers, Thomas, Robertson (who became a considerable Liverpool figure), and John, nor his sister Helen, who disgraced the family by taking to drugs and Catholicism (she converted in 1842). His older sister, Agnes, was a significant religious influence upon him. John Gladstone, the father, concurred in his wife's Evangelicalism and believed in a devout, God-fearing household, but within that limitation he permitted a remarkable freedom of discussion to his children. In many ways William seemed to have had a merry childhood, although he chose to remember it in a mood of Evangelical gloom: "I have no recollection of being a loving or a winning child: or an earnest or diligent or knowledge-loving child."[2] Having made a fortune by following his own bent and not being bound by old-fashioned mercantile notions, John Gladstone allowed a similar sort of adventuresomeness in thinking at home—the children could dispute almost anything. This was to have its bad effect upon William; in later life he would irritate many of his contemporaries by being incurably disputatious and argumentative, and unwilling to accept anything, or state anything, without endless qualifications. The intensity and number of disputes he enjoyed within his family circle—amicable, enjoyable disputes, for it was a happy family—did not prepare him to accept intellectual defeat and tended to blunt his judgment of character in the world outside. His fights throughout his life were conducted with intense emotion of the sort often associated with family life, and he treated most of his opponents in much the same way as he might have treated his brothers, sisters, and parents: fondly, tolerantly, sometimes with annoyance; sure, though, of their essential affection and sympathy. He seemed to feel that he had only to make them understand the rightness of his argument to have them yield to it, and give up their own wrongheaded position. Believing this, he was insufficiently aware of the need to allow for subtleties and quirks of character, and the prejudices that inspire convictions.

Those early arguments in the family circle also had as their result an unwillingness on his part to accept any ideas as fixed and absolute, even his own, and he therefore kept the possibility of change and development within himself. He never lost this quality and encouraged it in his own children. John Morley, that freethinker, was quite shocked, the first time he dined with the Gladstone family, to hear the children shrilly shout at their father after he had made some statement, "It's a lie, it's a lie!"

His family environment had allowed Gladstone to think freely, but within the discipline of a firm religious creed and in a household dedicated to the practical business of the world. It would seem that everything in his early life conspired to set up a framework of uncommon rigidity in which to contain ideas and concepts of striking flexibility. This was even true in the political tradition of the Gladstone family. The father, as we have seen, was a devoted follower of George Canning, and though Canning died when William was eighteen, he was to be a profound influence upon the young man's political thinking (and perhaps upon his education, for Gladstone followed the same path, Eton and Christ Church, Oxford, as Canning had). In 1812 John Gladstone was instrumental in the election of Canning as M.P. for Liverpool. It was at a dinner at the Gladstone home, in front of Canning, that William delivered what he liked to call his maiden speech, at the age of two years and ten months. It consisted in its entirety of "Ladies and Gentlemen."

It is too easily assumed that Gladstone's life was marked by a move from a fierce and unrelenting Toryism to a benign Liberalism, but it was the vehemence with which he held his opinions rather than the opinions themselves that encourage this assumption. His early Toryism was very much in the style of Canning. Something of an outsider figure himself, Canning was associated with the younger group of Tories who, with the sympathy if not the understanding of Lord Liverpool, were attempting to revitalize their party. Gladstone's being a disciple of Canning meant that from the time he began to think about politics he believed in Catholic Emancipation. It also meant that he embarked on his career as a passionate enemy of radical political reform, while he adhered to Canning's, and later to Peel's, belief in the possibilities of administrative change.

As he grew older, he continued to revere those significant political figures whom he had admired in his youth and to hope that he was loyal to their ideas. Yet it was not in specific ideas but in certain fundamental attitudes that Canning had his most marked influence upon Gladstone. From Canning he derived his liberal attitude in foreign affairs: a conviction that nations had the right to assert their freedom. There was also the Canning-like belief in change within the established system, of tinkering with the traditional ways of doing things in order to improve society, with improvement seen in terms of maintaining a conservative world—although in Canning's case, as later in Gladstone's, the changes he advocated were likely to be so great that it became increasingly difficult to recognize the conservative implications of his policies.

The tradition of Canning—and of Burke, in whom

Gladstone had read widely—meant a belief in a mixed polity in which the interests of all classes would be considered and in some sense represented in Parliament, not just those of the rich, the propertied, and the wellborn. Gladstone's cast of mind was conservative. The figures who were crucial in shaping his thought—Aristotle, Augustine, Dante, Bishop Butler, Burke, Canning—were believers in order and hierarchy, but they also were believers in justice. Throughout his life Gladstone kept his mind open on the form that order should take; he never believed that society as it happened to be at the beginning of the nineteenth century was for the best in all possible worlds.

Canning's influence may also be recognized in Gladstone's awareness of the importance of public opinion: that a statesman must allow for such pressures upon him in shaping his policies. Gladstone seems not to have been sensitive to individual character, but he knew character in the mass—whether it was the mood of the House of Commons or of an audience in its thousands. He believed firmly that there was a moment at which a move should be made—when he felt himself "in tune" with his audience—an appropriate moment at which an idea should be put forward in the world.

Scotland; Evangelicalism; Liverpool and commerce; even Canningite conservatism—all these might be described as consistent with a middle-class background in early nineteenth century England, and they were important to Gladstone. Almost certainly they had the effect of making him sympathetic to the more progressive aspects of Victorian society. But even more important was the nature of his own experience. He could encompass so much, understand so much, in a social sense, of his century, because in his early years he had experienced a successful enactment of the aspirations (and fantasies) of so many members of the mercantile class: first by education, and then by marriage, he appeared to change class and position. The price, at the beginning of his career, was a certain rigidity in ideas and actions, and he seemed to have imbibed only the superficial Toryism of his idol, Canning; later, as he came into his own, it was evident that what had truly influenced him was Canning's imaginative and malleable conservatism.

His father sent him to Eton in 1821. There he was to know the closeness of growing up with the future rulers of England that has been described by Disraeli in *Coningsby,* and by many later writers. It was a time when the cult of sports had not yet established itself in the public schools, so that Gladstone, although undistinguished as an athlete, was able to be a leader. He was elected a member of the Eton Society, or "Pop," where issues of the world were debated, and he was coeditor of the *Eton Miscellany,* in whose pages, in 1827, he published the first effort of a long and prolific writing career.

The same year he was elected to "Pop," 1825, he also started his extraordinary diary, which is now being published as one of the most extensive documents of the nineteenth century. Mostly it consists of daily jottings about people seen and written to, and a record of his activities. But among its many, many pages there are sometimes revealing autobiographical glimpses, most particularly paragraphs of introspection when he finds himself unworthy, such assessments taking place most notably on his birthdays. In the early years of the diary, a concern with masturbation manifested itself. Indeed, all through the volumes so far published there is an intense preoccupation with sexuality, which later was evident in his obsession with pornography, his attempts to save prostitutes, and his self-flagellation when he questioned the purity of the motives of his rescue work.

If there was anything at Eton he regretted, it was the absence of religious conviction, for the tone of the school was not as earnest as it would become later in the century. But the pious young Gladstone was grateful for the religious forms that were observed, and upon which he depended in the attempt to make himself a better person. "The actual teaching of Christianity was all but dead, though happily none of its forms had been surrendered," he wrote when looking back upon his Eton days.

At Eton, and afterward at Christ Church, Oxford, where he went in 1828, he became familiar with the sons of gentry and nobility, who were expected in the nature of things to go on to rule England. Again and again his own experience would be repeated throughout the nineteenth century: the son of the businessman who was sent to Eton and one or other of the Ancient Universities and was assimilated to the ruling classes. Christ Church further polished Gladstone's *veneer* of conservatism. (One is reminded of Balfour's remark about him, that he could be a tremendous old Tory in everything but essentials.) At the same time, his own educational career made him aware of the gradual expansion of the traditional English governing class through its assimilation of newer groups. He also learned the manners and customs of the governing classes themselves. (As it happened, he first came to their notice as one of their most brilliant defenders.) Thanks to his education he acquired the advan-

tageous position of a son of the aristocracy, without losing his sense of sympathy and identification with the
commercial interests of his own family.

Oxford played an extremely important role in Gladstone's life, and he would always maintain the closest
and fondest connection with it. He represented it as its
M.P. from 1847 to 1865, when the university rejected
him because of his religious views, but in spite of this
rebuff, his loyalty to it continued undimmed over the
years. As late as 1890 he thoroughly enjoyed himself during a week's visit to All Souls. And when he was on his
deathbed he was deeply touched by a sympathetic message from the Hebdomadal Council, and slowly dictated
a reply of thanks for the "Christian sympathy" from the
"ancient university of Oxford, the God-fearing and God-
sustaining university of Oxford. I served her perhaps
mistakenly, but to the best of my ability." The begin-
nings of a strongly religious atmosphere at the university
when he was an undergraduate—the first stirrings of the
Oxford Movement—and to his delight, the range of brilliant sermons being offered, confirmed him in his already
profoundly religious temperament. But the tradition-
alism of Oxford ultimately conflicted with Gladstone's
views. An elderly Whig remarked when hearing an early
speech of his on the Budget, "Ah, Oxford on the surface,
but Liverpool below." As G. M. Young observes, Gladstone's development consisted of his "long slow journey
back from Oxford to Liverpool."[3]

He did not lose his more northern, middle-class qualities while exposed to a serious yet upper-class education.
Rather, he maintained a very uneasy alliance of all his
tendencies. He did brilliantly at Oxford. Academically,
he secured, as Peel had done, a double first in classics and

mathematics. Politically, he was very active. He witnessed the debate at Convocation over an anti-Catholic petition in 1829, which led to Peel's resigning his seat for the university; and as a supporter of Catholic Emancipation, he was aware from the very beginning that he was not as dyed-in-the-wool a conservative as Oxford might like. Yet he opposed the possibility of radical political reform, maintaining his loyalty to the conservative principles of Canning and Burke. He claimed in 1865 that "the Reform bill frightened me in 1831, and drove me off my natural and previous bias. Burke and Canning misled many on that subject, and they misled me."[4] But it may well be that he was attempting to impose an excessive consistency upon the history of his ideas. His campaign against Reform, which included local canvasing, during which he was jostled by mobs, also brought him to the attention of the university at large. He spoke against Reform in the Union on May 17, 1831, so impressively that his hearers felt that they were listening to a future Prime Minister. Of course such thoughts must frequently go through the minds of the young, proud and hopeful of themselves and of their contemporaries, but it is pleasant, and alarmingly frequent at Oxford, when such expectations are fulfilled. Among those who had been impressed by the speech was Lord Lincoln, the eldest son of the Duke of Newcastle, who would arrange for his father to offer to Gladstone his political interest at Newark a year later.

By the time he entered Parliament, at the age of twenty-three, after his experience at Eton and Oxford, and a grand tour, Gladstone had assimilated himself to the highest echelons of English society. Nonetheless he kept a certain distance from "society" and regarded it with a degree of aloofness. In these early years it was primarily through his religion that he maintained his individuality: Evangelicalism was more common among the merchant class from which he came than among the aristocracy, and he felt his religion so keenly that he wished in 1830 to dedicate his life to the Church, but his father would not allow it. He conceived of his life as dedicated to God; politics were a second-best way of trying to achieve a more Christian community. He would sooner hear a sermon than see a sight, and he did not allow his career to interfere with his churchgoing. In his youth he had a tendency to be narrow-minded in an Evangelical fashion, but he was not unbending—he played cards (though not without qualms), he never opposed drink, and he would, if he must, travel on the Sabbath. In 1832, forced to visit his constituency on a Sunday, he regretted the journey, and wrote of it in his journal: "Conversation with a tory countryman who got in [the coach] for a few miles, on Sunday travelling, which we agreed in disapproving. Gave him some tracts." But already by this time his religious views were being modified, and he was arriving at that somewhat odd combination of attitudes which made him sympathetic to, and able to represent, more than one of the religious currents of the century. He would never lose his Evangelicalism, his Evangelical's belief in the importance of the individual and of individual effort. But while on his grand tour, he was much impressed—especially in St. Peter's, and again in Naples—by the Catholic Church as an institution. He felt drawn toward the idea of the primacy of the Church, and somewhat away from the primary importance, as taught by Evangelicalism, of the Bible. Gladstone became "ecumenical" early; it was in St. Peter's on March 31,

1832, that he had his first conception of the fundamental unity of the Church and felt a wish to work for its attainment. All through his life he had an ambivalent relation to Catholicism. He was extremely fond of such eminent Catholics as Acton and Döllinger. Yet he was profoundly disturbed when his sister Helen and his close friend Henry Manning became Catholics. He could, thus, both identify with the pervasive anti-Catholicism of nineteenth-century England, and remain sympathetic to Catholic feeling itself, most notably in Ireland. In his own views he managed to hold in balance throughout his life elements of Evangelicalism and High Churchmanship and believed in their relevance to his public activities. As he wrote to Manning in 1835, "Politics would become an utter blank to me were I to make the discovery that we were mistaken in maintaining their association with religion."

This combination of religious views first manifested itself in his early twenties, when he was beginning his political career as a protégé of the Duke of Newcastle, and when his adult character was emerging. He had survived the tensions imposed upon him, first by the freedom of his upbringing within its framework of strictness, then by the slight but highly significant contrasts between his social position and his education, and finally by his frustration in the choice of a career. Religion provided the means for Gladstone to tame the "impetuous, irrestrainable, uncontrollable" side of his character. (But he derived much of his power and passion from this side; and it may also account for the changes of direction in his policies, the verbiage of his speeches, and his occasional lassitude when faced with the need for action.) It was at this time, or so Mrs. Gladstone told John Morley when he was working on the official biography, that Gladstone conquered these characteristics "through the natural strength of his character and constant wrestling in prayer."⁵ As Philip Magnus suggests in his biography, Gladstone's aim was to reduce the world to a sense of religious order such as he had achieved for himself in his own character. While he never departed from his belief that religion was man's most important concern, his concept of the relation of religion and politics became increasingly liberal, and more flexible, as he grew older. He eventually came to the conclusion that the State could best serve religion by freeing the Church from the State. It was almost as if in his personal life he liberalized his concept of religion to the degree that he felt that his personality no longer needed the restraints and otherworldly rewards of religion, although he never ceased to be deeply devout.

In 1839 Gladstone married Catherine Glynne, a relationship that enriched his life immeasurably, while continuing to add to it new elements of contrast. He had been looking for a wife since 1835, and characteristically he had set his sights high—first he had turned his attention to Caroline Farquhar, a sister of a school friend and the daughter of Sir Thomas Farquhar, and then two years later toward Lady Frances Douglas, daughter of the Earl of Morton. Both these attractive young ladies were put off by his earnestness, his obsession with religion, and they simply felt no love for him. He was fortunate that they put him off, for in Catherine Glynne he found his perfect match. Mrs. Gladstone was an extraordinary woman, impulsive, generous, absolutely dedicated to her husband, although at times she was a little impatient at his wordiness—once she remarked, "Oh, William dear, if you weren't such a great man you would be a terrible bore." But she was more likely to say, as she did once on hearing him speak, "In point of *treat* the hearing you is ever to me like listening to beautiful, sweet music." Theirs was a completely happy marriage, and Mrs. Gladstone's attitude toward her husband is perhaps best summed up in another remark: "I never can make him think himself a great man! Which everyone else thinks, or should think."[6]

It was a grand marriage for Gladstone in every sense. He married into the distinguished family of the Glynnes, the greatest landowners in Flintshire, and related to a goodly number of Whig aristocrats. (The latter were an important element in the party he would eventually join, and from which they would eventually withdraw, in large part because of Gladstone and his policies.) His association with the land, which he took very seriously, and its hierarchical society, strengthened his conservative tendencies and encouraged his sense of order so necessary for himself and for his world. Hawarden, the Glynne house, provided a firm base, worth considerable effort of preserving, fixed in its values, and from which he could venture upon new and radical schemes.

The relationship of Gladstone to his estate by marriage illustrates much about his life—he so identified with it that many thought it was his own family inheritance. Actually, his father was landless, but he was so successful that he was able to acquire considerable acreage, most notably the large estate of Fasque in Scotland. Gladstone was quite irrationally irritated that in 1851—on his father's death—the estate was left, as was customary, to the eldest son, his brother Thomas, and not to himself, even though he was the most prominent member of the family. (The present owner of Hawarden, Sir William Gladstone, the Prime Minister's great-grandson, has, through the dying out of the senior line of the family, become the owner both of Hawarden and Fasque.)

Considering the degree to which Gladstone was held to be responsible for the weakening of the landed classes, it is impressive, and ironic, to discover how important he held that class to be and what considerable efforts he expended to make sure that his brother-in-law's estate would be preserved. His spirit certainly still dominates the village of Hawarden, just a few miles from Chester, across the Welsh border in Flintshire, and practically in view of Liverpool. There, in the center, is the statue of Gladstone himself, surrounded by figures representing Ireland, Classical Learning, Finance, and Eloquence. Behind his statue is St. Deniol's Library. Having changed with the times it is no longer dedicated to men pursuing divine studies, but is open to all who wish a place to read, surrounded by many books from Gladstone's library, supplemented over the years. Next door is the church, where many of the Gladstones are buried in the churchyard. William and Catherine Gladstone themselves are buried in Westminster Abbey. Within the church, however, are recumbent figures of the Gladstones in an elaborate memorial chapel, designed by Sir William Richmond; the west window is a memorial to William Gladstone—the last work designed by Sir Edward Burne-Jones. The gates of the park open to the center of the village, and there one can proceed to the house, Hawarden Castle, much as it was in Gladstone's day. In the Temple of Peace one can still see his spectacles, his walking sticks, the axes with which he chopped down trees—and even a few chips from the trees themselves tied in ribbons. There is also a small, adjoining domed room with perfect acoustics in which he could, if he so wished, rehearse speeches for the House of Commons or for out-of-doors. At Hawarden he achieved one of his desires—to be identified with a village—odd though that may have seemed to the many who regarded him as a destroyer of the older rural British values.

His life on the estate can be taken to stand for the paradox of much of his career: he firmly believed in the value of land and in the landed proprietor, yet a good deal of his legislative activity worked to the detriment of both. In Gladstone's day twenty-five hundred people dwelt on the estate of some seven thousand acres, producing in 1876 an income of approximately £18,000 from wheat and coal. It was the largest estate in the smallest county in Wales, and the Glynnes had owned it since the mid-seventeenth century, although they did not take up residence there until the early eighteenth century.

The most famous consequence of Gladstone's coming into control of the estate is that he was able to preserve it. His brother-in-law, Sir Stephen Glynne, had launched a manufacturing enterprise of iron and steel on a family property, Oak Farm, in Staffordshire. The firm overexpanded and went bankrupt in 1847—the estate had been pledged to support the enterprise and Oak Farm was in debt to the extent of £450,000. Gladstone saved the estate by pouring his own inheritance into it, a little less than £300,000. He always felt that this was invaluable experience for his career, once remarking, "It supplied in fact my education for the office of finance Minister," and it is true that he might not have had direct financial experience of both land and factory if he had not married into the Glynne family. He did not acquire the estate in his own name until 1874, upon the death of his two brothers-in-law—and characteristically he then handed the estate over to his eldest son, although he continued to be its controlling figure until his own death. Whatever his detractors might claim, he did not contemplate any basic changes in the landed system. As he remarked to his tenants in 1890, "Upon the whole, I am inclined to believe that the best and most wholesome system is that which now prevails, the well-working of which depends upon the wisdom and good conduct of the people concerned, where the soil is owned by one set of men, and occupied and cultivated by another set of men."[7]

It can be said that in many ways Gladstone's first thirty years were devoted to imposing a conservative overlay upon his mercantile and Evangelical background, to making himself a powerful, if at times uneasy, combination of outsider and insider. His first election, at Newark in December 1832, confirmed this pattern. He ran as an anti-Reform candidate, in which position he agreed with his patron, the Duke of Newcastle, but there was also a point of disagreement—the Duke was an anti-Canningite. It was a hard battle within a considerable electorate of 1,600, of whom 1,200 were working-class. Gladstone's problem was to unseat the Whig member who had been elected against the Duke's interest, as the Duke only controlled about one quarter of the votes.

The program Gladstone issued suggests to what degree he was conservative—he wanted the continuation of the union of Church and State, particularly in Ireland—but there were slightly more modern attitudes in his desire for the improvement of the Poor Laws, and even in a

somewhat ambiguous statement about the need for more
education for slaves in order to prepare them for emancipation. This latter position was not positive enough for
the antislavery men who fought him in the constituency,
but it was some distance for him to go considering that
his father owned slaves in the West Indies.

He spent three months campaigning in Newark, in a
hotly contested and corrupt election on the eve of the
Reform Bill. Not until after it was over did Gladstone
discover how much the election had cost the Duke and his
father, who had put up half the money; the corruption
disturbed him, even though it meant that he had come
out head of the poll, and so was launched upon his political career.

It was a career that was to extend over a period of
sixty-one years, in the course of which he would deliver
some two thousand speeches, most of them in the House
of Commons, beginning on June 3, 1833 (his first major
speech), and ending on May 4, 1897, with a talk at Hawarden. The total is formidable, indeed almost incredible, but Gladstone was unceasingly prolific. One must
never forget the range of his genius, his extraordinary
capacities, his knowledge of many languages, his interests
in theology and literature, in Biblical and classical scholarship. His own voluminous writings range from the first
contributions in the *Eton Miscellany* in 1827 to two
articles in 1898, the year of his death, one on the housing
of books, and, as though to frame his life, some personal
recollections of his great friend at Eton, Arthur Hallam.

At St. Deniol's Library can be found thirty-eight stout
volumes of printed speeches and pamphlets, put together
by his friends Sir Robert and Lady Phillimore. The flow

from his pen was prodigious: he gathered his own miscellany in eight volumes of *Gleanings,* as well as many volumes of scholarship and speeches.

In May 1897, at Hawarden, a year before his death, he gave his last major talk, "The Condition of the Clergy," and some of his most famous speeches were those he gave in public: particularly in the Midlothian campaigns of the late 1870's. They were in large part responsible for recasting the nature of the conduct of politics in England. But his aim, even in his public speeches, was always to influence Parliament and his party, rather than the public itself. Thanks to cheaper newspapers and increased literacy, public addresses were being read by more and more people, and this was true also of speeches delivered in Parliament. The latter were the most immediately important politically of Gladstone's speeches, and from among them I have selected a number for particular consideration as one way to encompass his extraordinary career.

Gladstone's prolixity sometimes irritated his contemporaries; it has irritated his biographers; and it continues to irritate. It is true that his speeches at their worst abound in endless qualifications. Perhaps the tensions, argumentativeness, and contrasts that marked his early life and education led him to oversubtle qualifications and discriminations. Perhaps he regarded such qualifications as a means of obtaining preciseness as well as offering ways of escape in the future, should he change his mind on an issue. As early as his Oxford days, when he was bracketed second in the Ireland Prize competition, the examiners found his papers "desultory beyond belief." He loved sermons, an inheritance from his Presbyterian forebears, and had a notable stamina for listening to and delivering them. He would improve his oratory by reading sermons aloud, and he also read from the Bible, and from his old favorites Homer, Aristotle, Augustine, Dante, and Bishop Butler. Given his love of language, his enjoyment of amplification, antitheses, parallels, abstract nouns, word pairs, compound adjectives, adverbs and verbs, it meant that he rarely said anything in the most concise way possible. Early in his career he asked Peel whether or not he should be short and concise when speaking on an issue, and Peel replied, "No, be long and diffuse. It is all important in the House of Commons to state your case in many different ways, so as to produce an effect on men of many ways of thinking." Or, as John Bright remarked about Gladstone's style of speaking, he "seldom sailed boldly from headland to headland; he preferred to hug the coast, and to follow to its source any navigable river which he encountered during his voyage." But it was this very quality which gave his speeches their richness, and copiousness. Granting that in print they do not convey the power of his voice, his piercing eye, which captivated Parliament and stirred a crowd with emotion and conviction, there is no question that Gladstone's speeches were often grand and elevating, nor that they remain of crucial importance in determining the form and substance of his politics.

ONE

Slavery
June 3, 1833

As a Canningite Tory, Gladstone was admirably suited for flexibility, and if the particular issues with which he made his mark at the beginning of his career had been matters of foreign policy, or of finance, its eventual course might have been less surprising. As it was, he was unable in his first years in Parliament, through a combination of circumstances, to avoid declaring himself on issues where his own family loyalties and religious beliefs were at stake. He felt forced to take rigid positions that were very different from those he would adopt on similar issues many years later.

He entered the House of Commons as a Tory at the end of 1832, in the first Reformed Parliament. Although he made several brief interventions in the early months of 1833 (in his official maiden speech on February 21, 1833, he had defended Lord Sandon's election as an M.P. for Liverpool), his first considerable speech, a crucial event in a parliamentarian's career, was made on June 3, 1833. In the course of a debate on slavery he responded to an attack by the Whig leader, Lord Howick. To under-

stand the position that Gladstone adopted, it is only necessary to recall that his father's business interests had
extended into the West Indies, where he had acquired
estates and become a slave owner on a considerable scale.
These interests of the Gladstone family were sufficient to
keep Gladstone, a devoted son, from joining with other
Evangelicals in agitating for the abolition of the institution of slavery in 1833 (the trade in slaves had been abolished in 1807). Some months earlier, in his election address, he had dealt with the point by making the standard
valid yet evasive reply of the conservative under attack—
look to your own house!—and it was true that a fair number of those who could afford the time and means to be
involved in the agitation against slavery were themselves
employers of "wage slaves." And he went on to claim, not
unjustly, that child employees were less well taken care
of than many a slave—the argument is familiar. But even
then Gladstone must have been aware that there was a
fundamental difference between being slave and being
free.

Years afterward, when he had come to believe that the
greatest of virtues was liberty, he reread his first major
speech and felt that it was not satisfactory, and certainly
his assessment would be true if it were measured against
the position on slavery that he would ultimately hold.
Yet it is a very fine performance for an early effort, delivered at the age of twenty-three, and with that air of
authority that an experience of Eton and Oxford will
sometimes impart; and its content too (as distinct from
its manner) will repay study.

It was on the personal point, which the Whigs had not
neglected to emphasize (as both William and his brother
Thomas were in the House of Commons at the same

time), that Gladstone spoke. John Gladstone owned slaves; and it was claimed that there was an exact ratio between the profits of a sugar estate and the misery of the slaves. Thus, the Gladstones were painted as the crassest of materialists in the working of their estate on Demerara in British Guiana. William Gladstone's sense of probity, notable throughout his life, was evident in almost the very first words of this maiden speech: "It [is] a charge affecting moral character, for what man's character would not be affected if he should see, from the reports on his estate, that while the sugar cultivation was increasing, his slaves were dying off in equal proportion, and if, under such circumstances, he should continue the same system of management?" The burden of the speech was to disprove the charge: he maintained that there was no brutality in the treatment of slaves, at least on the Gladstone estates, and added that if there were brutality, then there would be no question that the property of the slave owners—that is, the slaves themselves—would be forfeit. Even in this first speech he revealed his extraordinary command of figures, and contradicted the contentions about numbers, and the conclusions drawn from them, that had been brought in the charge against his family. He demonstrated that there was not the correlation implied between production and loss of life, or punishment and loss of life, although he admitted that the cultivation of sugar was less healthy than that of cotton or coffee: "Sugar [is] best grown in damp soils: and in such, of course, more decomposition and putrefaction [takes] place under a tropical sun; and it [is] consequently less favourable to life." But he pointed out quite correctly that particular trades were not relinquished because they were more dangerous to life than other trades; or, using another

argument, that if "the manufacture of sugar [is] so essential and necessarily destructive, [the House] ought not to
stop till [it] had passed a law prohibiting its importation
altogether. . . . The extent of injury to life from many
even of the most ordinary trades in this country [is] almost beyond belief, and far [exceeds] the effects of the
cultivation of sugar."

The bulk of the speech was devoted to attacking the
logic and supporting figures of his opponents in order
to protect the interests of the slave-owning West Indians.
Yet even in this case, when Gladstone appeared at his
most conservative, he did not try to hide completely from
himself that there was a moral issue involved, not merely
in regard to his own family, but in the question of the
institution of slavery itself. His tone, however, was at a
slight remove, even as his argumentation was slightly dis-
ingenuous; yet he left little doubt that he was in favor of
the emancipation of the slaves. (Such a position was not
inconsistent with the interests of the slave owners; they
knew that slavery was doomed.) The real question before
the House had to do with the form of apprenticeship and
compensation: "Cases of wanton cruelty [have] occurred;
and they always [will] exist, particularly under the system
of slavery; and unquestionably this [is] a substantial reason why the British Legislature and public should set
themselves in good earnest to provide for its extinction;
but these cases of cruelty [can] easily be explained by the
West Indians, who [represent] them as rare and isolated
cases, and who [maintain] that the ordinary relation of
master and slave [is] one of kindliness and not of hostility." But Gladstone himself made no effort to tem-
porize that cruelty, whether on a large or small scale, was
intolerable. "It [is] abhorrent to the nature of English-

men," he declared, speaking with the voice of the English moralist. But in his very next phrase he spoke with the voice of the English businessman: "Conceding all these things, [are] not Englishmen to retain a right to their own honestly and legally acquired property?" The contradiction between the two voices would not be reconciled in this youthful speech . . . perhaps he had not yet come to understand that it was in fact irreconcilable.

One further aspect of this early effort deserves comment. In a curious fashion it may be said to anticipate the future course of Gladstone's thinking. He is making for the first time a point that he would make again later from a more liberal point of view. Even as a young man he had a highly developed sense of the importance of trade, and recognized that the colonies, as more and more of Europe became industrialized, might well play an increasingly large part in sustaining British prosperity. He also knew—after all, the experience of the American Revolution was not so far in the past—that it was necessary in any such step as the emancipation of the slaves to have the cooperation of the men in the colony itself—to have, in effect, some form, no matter how limited, of "Home Rule": "Whilst the competition of foreign manufacturers [is] daily becoming more formidable, it [may] be by the colonies, and by the colonies alone, that the country [may] yet flourish. For passive resistance and for the production of evil the power of the local Legislature [is] immense. The House [may] consume its time and exert its wisdom in devising plans of emancipation; but without the concurrence of the Colonial Legislatures, success [will] be hopeless."

He ended this first important speech of his with an eloquent peroration, restating a standard conservative principle: that not everyone was ready for the step about to be taken. (Later he would turn it around to make it a liberal principle: that individuals should be given as much freedom as they are prepared for.) And he suggested, in good Burkean form, that the rights of those with responsibilities and property must not be disregarded. In all but the most fleeting way, he avoided passing any judgment upon the institution of slavery itself. Yet the speech cannot be taken, as it sometimes has been in retrospect, as a defense of slavery. Rather he was defending the interests of the planters in the considerable investment they had made in property—a point that would have carried more impressive weight if the property in question had not been *human* property. The voice of the businessman and the voice of the moralist did not blend harmoniously. He concluded:

> It is the duty of the House to place as broad a distinction as possible between the idle and the industrious slaves, and nothing [can] be too strong to secure the freedom of the latter; but, with respect to the idle slaves, no period of emancipation [can] hasten their improvement. If the labours of the House [are to] be conducted to a satisfactory issue, it [will] redound to the honour of the nation and to the reputation of his Majesty's Ministers, whilst it would be delightful to the West-India planters themselves, for they must always feel, that to hold in bondage their fellow men must always involve the greatest responsibility. But let not any man think of carrying this measure by force. England rested her power not upon physical force, but upon her principles, her intellect, and virtue; and if this great measure were not placed on a fair basis, or were conducted by violence, [I] should lament it, as a

signal for the ruin of the colonies, and the downfall of the empire.[1]

Yet for all his air of assurance when he addressed the House, the young Gladstone had mixed feelings about the issue of slavery; it did not lend itself to merely reasonable argument. Two months later, when William Wilberforce, the emancipator of the slaves, died, Gladstone noted in his diary: "Attended Mr. Wilberforce's funeral. It brought solemn thoughts, particularly about the slaves. That is a burdensome question."[2]

TWO

Religion
February 4, 1845

IN HIS EARLY YEARS Gladstone took the conservative side on almost every domestic issue. He was in favor of repressive measures to maintain order in Ireland; against admitting Jews to Parliament; against admitting Dissenters to Oxford and Cambridge; against the abolition of flogging in the army; and in favor of maintaining military sinecures.

As at Oxford, his views and his abilities brought him to the attention of those who led the Tory party, and in December 1834 he was made a Junior Lord of the Treasury in Sir Robert Peel's newly formed Government: his career was following an aristocratic rather than a mercantile pattern. As one M.P. said to him, "You are about the youngest lord who was ever placed at the treasury on his own account, and not because he was his father's son."[1] Only a month later, after the General Election, he was made Undersecretary for War and the Colonies. He had just turned twenty-five. This was the Government appointed on the behest of William IV, the last time a monarch would take such an initiative, and it was in office for only four months.

But despite the brevity of this first experience of office, Gladstone continued to be active in politics. And he began to be active, too, as a writer.

In 1838, he published *The State in Its Relations with the Church,* growing out of his firm conviction that the purpose of the State was to serve religion, specifically, the Church of England as by law established. The Church, he argued, was obligated to serve as the stern conscience of the English State; and the State, in turn, must distinguish between truth and error in religion. The book in which he elaborated upon this argument was the first and the most uncompromising of the great efforts he made throughout his life to relate the State to Christianity.[2] Here, even more than over the slavery issue, Gladstone branded himself as an intransigent, seemingly incapable of adapting to the utilitarianism of the time, and out of touch even with the Evangelicalism of his youth, which was less concerned with institutions than with individuals. It was as if he were overassimilated to the institutional prejudices of Oxford, and in a sense the book was Gladstone's own contribution to the Oxford Movement, a testament to his view of the overriding position and importance of the Church in men's lives. There is no question that he truly believed what he wrote; but it is also true that in writing it he subordinated (almost to the vanishing point) the more liberal elements in his character—which existed even then—with the consequence that his later life looks to be much more of a transformation than it actually was. The impact of the book was immediate. Thomas Babington Macaulay established the prevailing view when he wrote in the April 1839 number of the *Edinburgh Review* that Gladstone, as a politician and as an author, was "the rising hope of those stern and unbending Tories who follow, reluctantly and mutinously, a leader [Peel] whose experience and eloquence are indispensable to them, but whose cautious temper and moderate opinions they abhor." Macaulay's review did not diminish the book's popularity; in fact it went into two further editions.

Throughout his life—as testified in practically every word he wrote—Gladstone saw himself as dedicated to religion. That commitment was at its most explicit in his early years. We have seen how at Oxford he had wished to enter the priesthood—one trembles to think what might have happened to the Church of England if he had become Archbishop of Canterbury. In January 1832, while staying with his parents during vacation, he felt it necessary to write, rather than to speak to, his father about his "call." Gladstone senior objected strenuously and the son in the end acceded to his father's wish that he abandon the idea of a life in the Church and enter politics instead. But his purpose in politics would be to defend the Church. The shift in vocation might well have represented a struggle within himself, externalized as a conflict with his father. After all, at Eton he had written out visiting cards for himself as the "Rt. Hon. William E. Gladstone, M.P." One suspects that his original bent was in the direction of politics. But, characteristically, he felt that he had to aim for higher things. Also characteristically, he felt guilty about giving in to his father—if he had held to his position to enter the Church, would not his father have yielded?[3]

Gladstone, in writing *The State in Its Relations with the Church,* was attempting to instill into his political career the fervor of the religious life that he had wished for and relinquished in 1830. Peel himself thought the book very much a false step. As a practical and brilliant politician, he felt that so forthright a declaration of principle, when not called for, was unwise. He remarked to Richard Monckton Milnes, who himself had chosen literature over politics, that he could not understand why a young man like Gladstone, with a brilliant political career before him, would bother to write books.

What Peel could not be expected to appreciate was that Gladstone was a herald of the new seriousness. He was far removed from the sort of practicality that marked the politicians who had come to maturity in the first decades of the century. Yet he was not at all unworldly; he was well endowed with the energy and thoroughness essential to a politician, though they had still to be translated into ways that would prove of the greatest political effectiveness.

It was also the period in which he was learning about finance. One of Peel's great contributions to English politics was to train a group of brilliant administrators who would help their country cope with the growing problems of a modern society. When Peel came into office in 1841, he appointed Gladstone Vice-President of the Board of Trade. Two years later, at the age of thirty-three, Gladstone was brought into the Cabinet as President. In both posts he did important work, moving England toward free trade and discovering practical ways of dealing with the new developments—such as the railroads—that the Industrial Revolution had brought into being. (And he was very much the shrewd Liverpool man of business, enforcing economies and determined to save the State halfpennies.) But the curious and perverse delicacy of his mind still manifested itself. Before deciding to enter the Cabinet, he had a long talk with Peel to make clear his belief in the need for dividing the bishoprics of Bangor and St. Asaph, a comparatively minor point of difference from the Government policy, about which he had scruples. Two devout friends, Manning and the barrister James Hope-Scott, both at that time within the Church of England, though both would later become Catholics, persuaded him that such minor hesitations were not sufficient cause for him to stay out of the Cabinet.

A year later, however, those scruples caught up with him. At the end of 1844 he decided that he must resign from the Cabinet when the Government proposed to increase its annual grant to Maynooth, a Catholic training college in Ireland. Paradoxically, he now no longer objected to such an increase. But he felt compelled to keep himself consistent with his book on State and Church—wherein he had maintained that it was illegitimate for the State to support any but the established Anglican religion—and on January 28 resigned from the Cabinet.

By expiating his feeling through so drastic an action he purged himself from any further refined conceptions about the Church. He was now able to become a more accommodating and practical politician—assuming that anybody would trust him with office again! This quixotic act, it would seem, had freed him from excessively strict interpretations of his obligations. He had begun his liberation, and his move towards liberalism, through an act which on the surface appeared to be the most retrogressive step he could take. In later years he recognized that he had acted foolishly, that his action had been "fitter for a dreamer, or possibly a schoolman, than for the active purposes of public life in a busy and moving age."[4] Indeed, once he had resigned from the Cabinet, he would not even oppose the Bill that had incited his resignation; he voted in favor of it on its second reading in Parliament.

On February 4, 1845, in Parliament he made a public explanation of his act of resignation. In the twelve years since his speech on slavery, which was relatively clear-cut in its balanced argumentation, Gladstone had learned a lot, not all to the good. His style may have become even more disputatious and potentially even more unclear. He was now dealing with a very delicate situation, in which he wished to make fine distinctions, so much so that his listeners were not at all sure why he was resigning. Richard Cobden, the great agitator in favor of free trade, remarked about the speech: "What a marvellous talent is this, here have I been sitting listening with pleasure for an hour to his explanation, and yet I know no more why he left the government than before he began."[5]

In the course of the speech, Gladstone argued himself step by step into what he considered a logical position— a move forward from the position he had held at the time of his resignation. Thus, it can be said, resigning was the leap into the future necessary for a fresh start. In his speech on slavery he had put forward the case for and against the planters in a straightforward fashion even though he had family ties to them. Now, oddly, he was much more hesitant, at least on the surface, about disclosing the personal reasons that had led him to resign. He put himself forward only in a rather convoluted prose that concealed as much as it revealed:

> My object in offering myself to the House [to speak] is, to give an explanation of what relates more immediately to myself. I should not, however, venture upon such a step if it were not that I feel the acts of public men to be acts in which the public at large have a great concern; and therefore, although it be irksome and offensive to detain a public assembly charged with high functions by matters in which self occupies too prominent a position, my purpose is, in point of fact, to remove misunderstandings and misapprehensions which, without some explanation, might exist, and which, relating to others as well as myself, might prejudicially affect the public interests.

He then went on:

> I have felt myself placed in a situation in which it is difficult to reconcile apparently conflicting duties. On the one hand, I freely and entirely recognize the claim of this House to be informed, and to be fully and rightly informed, of the motives which lead Members of the House either to accept office under the Crown, or to undertake the scarcely less grave responsibility of quitting it; and, therefore, I cannot refuse to attempt giving some account of what has recently occurred with respect to myself. On the other hand, I feel that great inconvenience would arise if I were to attempt any detailed exposition having reference, as must necessarily be the case, to measures which have not yet come under the consideration of Parliament. I shall, therefore, endeavour to state, simply and frankly, the motives which have actuated me in the step to which I

have had recourse. But here I must appeal specially to the indulgence of the House, to receive what I have to say, not as a controversial statement, not as an argumentative defence, but merely as a representation which I trust will suffice to prevent misapprehension that might be mischievous, and yet will not lead to the premature discussion of subjects regarding which much angry feeling might perhaps be awakened. . . . I have acted according to what appeared to me to be the exigency of the case, and what was demanded by my own position, which I felt to be in some respects different from that of other Members of the Government. . . . I have not resigned on account of the intentions of the Government, so far as I have a knowledge of its intentions, with regard to any matter affecting the Church of England or the Church of Ireland. The cause, then, I am about to lay before the House is the sole cause which has led to the step I have adopted. And now again, I am driven to the necessity of adverting to myself, and to what I have said and done in former days. I have taken upon myself, some years ago, whether wisely or unwisely is not now the question, to state to the world, and that in a form the most detailed and deliberate, not under the influence of momentary consideration, nor impelled by the heat and pressure of debate, but in a published treatise, the views which I entertained on the subject of the relation of a Christian State to Religion and to the Christian Church. Of all subjects, therefore, which could be raised for public consideration, this, in its ultimate results at least the most important, I have treated in a manner the most detailed and deliberate. I have never, indeed, been guilty of the folly which has been charged upon me by some, of holding that there are any theories of political affairs, even in this their highest department, which are to be regarded alike under all circumstances as inflexible and immutable. But on the other hand, I have a strong conviction, speaking under ordinary circumstances, and as a general rule, that those who have thus borne the most solemn testimony to a particular view of a great constitutional question, ought not to be parties responsible for proposals which involve a material departure from them. . . . I am sensible how infirm my judgment is in all matters, and how easily I might have erred in one so complex as this, and involving the balance of so many and such different considerations. But still it has been my conviction, that although I was not to fetter my discretion as a Member of Parliament by a reference to theories which it had become impossible to realize, yet on the other hand it was absolutely due to the public, due to my public character, due to those terms on which alone general confidence can be reposed in public men, that I should under such circumstances, and in so important a matter, place myself, so far as in me lay, in a position to form not only an honest, but likewise an independent and an unsuspected judgment.

He was most anxious not to cast any aspersions upon his colleagues. He did not, in fact, disagree with their actions, but he felt that he could not be a party to increasing the support for the training of Roman Catholic seminarians in Ireland. He also anticipated in the same speech his future position, managing to suggest even in this most personal and idiosyncratic of statements what direction his ideas would take. He never changed his mind that in his ideal world there would be one Church and that the main role of the State would be to support it, and to serve the cause of religion. Even though at this moment of his life he was taking the most extreme step he would ever take on behalf of his concept of the ideal relation between Church and State, he seemed also to acknowledge in the very same speech that so perfect a world could not be achieved. And since this was the case, then there was no legitimate basis for discrimination: Catholics, Jews, Nonconformists—all were entitled to the aid and sustenance of the State. Two years later, he amazed those "stern and unbending" Tories by voting in favor of Bills to grant relief to Roman Catholics and to admit Jews to Parliament. Such steps were consistent with being a Canningite Tory, and with what he had said —if anyone had understood him—in convoluted paragraphs explaining his resignation:

> I can understand, and I have even ventured to vindicate, as the most excellent and true, in a state of society able to appreciate its truth, the principle upon which a Christian State allies itself for religious purposes with the Christian Church, and with the Christian Church alone; but if the time has come when, owing to the great advance of religious divisions, and likewise owing to a very great modification of political sentiments, what remains of that system must be further infringed, then I cannot undertake to draw any line of distinction unfavourable to my Roman Catholic fellow subjects in Ireland in particular. . . . I wish again, and most distinctly, to state that I am not prepared to take part in any religious warfare against that measure [to give more money to Maynooth]. . . . I wished to claim for myself prospectively, an entire liberty of judgment. . . . I have endeavoured to lay my motives frankly and fully before the House.[6]

This very speech, which appeared to be motivated by high-minded sectarian intolerance, in fact announced Gladstone's move away from the idea of the State as a dedicated supporter of religion to a less perfect yet freer idea. Six years later, on March 25, 1851, he would give one of his greatest speeches, a flowing speech, free of the baroque hesitations and complications of the apology for his resignation. The occasion was the second reading in the House of Commons of the Ecclesiastical Titles Assumption Bill, intended to prevent the Pope from giving English Catholic bishops territorial titles—the so-called papal aggression. The Bill, which reflected the pervasive anti-Catholic feelings of Parliament and the public, passed overwhelmingly, but had no effect: no Catholic bishops were prosecuted.

In his speech of 1851, Gladstone was to give a brilliant defense of religious liberty. It did not seem to bother him that he had resigned on an anti-Catholic position just six years earlier; nor does he hesitate to accuse Lord John Russell, the Prime Minister and progenitor of the Bill, a man associated with Whig theories of liberty and the Great Reform Bill, of inconsistency: "I ask you what you would have thought in the year 1845, if it had been foretold that the noble Lord would on the 25th of March, 1851, recommend to the House the second reading of a Bill to prohibit Roman Catholic ecclesiastics from bearing titles? How many men are there in this House who would have believed the prophecy if it had been made at the time? I do not think you could count them by units. I never heard a more impressive passage delivered by any speaker than one passage in the speech of the noble Lord upon the second reading of the Bill enlarging the endowment of the College of Maynooth." Some might think that Gladstone himself was being very inconsistent, but he was making, albeit more clearly, the same point in this speech that he had been implying in 1845—that the State must, if it is not going to devote itself exclusively to supporting the truth as found in the Church of England, treat all religions equally: "All I will observe is, if you fall back on the doctrine of supremacy in its highest and most rigid form, I protest, for one, against its unequal application. If it is applied to the Roman Catholics, let it be applied also to the Wesleyans and all other bodies. In my opinion, the universal sense of the House would revolt against such applications; therefore, do not extort from the ancient doctrine of supremacy a proposition which is unfavourable to religious liberty, and a partial and exceptional application to the case of the Roman Catholics." He went into a long historical disquisition to support his position, and toward its end he lamented that Hampden and Pym—those high-minded opponents of Charles I—should have been evoked by others in their least favorable aspect as anti-Catholics. The most important parts of his speech are those in which he cited principles of religious liberty, and urged his listeners not to turn backward: in effect, not to take up the position that he himself once held. He also felt that a welcoming of the so-called papal aggression would actually weaken the power of the Pope, for the bishops, replacing as they would vicars apostolic, would strengthen, Gladstone thought, the progressive, antipapal, more "democratic" aspects of the Catholic Church: "By the introduction of diocesan episcopates, you give scope to local principle, and to a class in the Roman Catholic Church, certain fixed and intelligible rights; thus tending, *pro tanto,* to attach them to yourselves, and to detach them from allegiance to the Pope." This might well have been a little optimistic, but it does demonstrate how he was capable of combining principles, such as that of religious freedom, with what he considered might be practical gains.

His main argument, however, was on the basis of religious liberty:

Will you go backwards or forwards in the career of religious freedom? Have you no faith in your free institutions? Do you think so ill of England—do you think so ill of the national character—do you think so ill of the capacity of your religion to bear the brunt of free competition, as to say you will now attempt to fence it about with legal enactments, instead of trusting to its own spiritual strength, and to the firmness and depth of your own convictions—above all, to this conviction, that, if the truth is on your side, God will give you the victory? . . . If I desert the broad and strong ground of principle that leads me to abide by the religious principles of all classes of the community —what security have I that other more formidable measures may not be in the background, and that for another half century the question of civil disqualification and religious liberty is not to absorb the time of the British Parliament, divide the minds of the British public, unseat Ministers, dissolve Parliaments, and interrupt the regular progress of civil legislation.

What an extraordinary transformation of his earlier view when he felt that the State should concern itself minutely with religious questions. Gladstone anticipated the divisive effects of sectarian feelings on legislation that would mark the century, although its most retarding effect was on education, in which he was never particularly interested. His final argument is now a truism about religious liberty, but was not regarded as such at the time. "We cannot turn back the tendencies of the age towards religious liberty. It is our business to forward them. To endeavour to turn them back is childish, and every effort you may make in that direction will recoil upon you with disaster and disgrace."[7]

The Ecclesiastical Titles Assumption Act in fact was a dead letter, and it was Gladstone's pleasure to see it repealed in 1871, during his own first ministry. He made a fast but thorough transformation from a man who was practically a religious bigot to a man of tolerance, and it was more than the equivocations of a schoolman by which he could claim that he held both positions with a belief in the importance of religion, but with different concepts of the role of the State in relation to religious truth. True religion would, he felt, have to conquer by its own efforts.

THREE

Foreign Policy
June 27, 1850

GLADSTONE DID NOT EXPECT that his resignation from the Cabinet in 1845 would be the effective prelude to many years outside either party, although he was not without office in the years to come. But it was not until 1859 that he was again firmly within a party, and then the Liberal not the Tory party; it was not until 1868, when he first became Prime Minister, that the two-party structure would have the same comparatively firm outline it had had in 1845. In December 1845, having made clear in his own mind his differences with the Government, he reentered the Cabinet as Colonial Secretary. Already he felt more strongly than Peel the necessity for free trade, and had moved in that direction as President of the Board of Trade. But with his customary excessive scrupulosity, he came to the conclusion that, given his opinion on free trade, he could not continue to sit as Member for Newark against what he considered the opinions of his constituents and under the patronage of the protectionist—that is, anti–free trade—Duke of Newcastle, even though Newcastle's eldest son, Lord Lincoln, did not hesitate to be a Minister, outside the Cabinet, in Peel's Government. So Gladstone sought another constituency, Oxford University—in which the voters were the M.A.'s of the university—which he would not outgrow in terms of his views for some eighteen years. He was not elected to Parliament again until August 1847, so he was in the odd position of being in the Cabinet from December 1845 until July 1846, but not in the House of Commons. Hence he had not been able to participate in the virulent debates over the repeal of the Corn Laws. Perhaps his relations with Disraeli would have been better in future years if he had had an opportunity to vent his feeling in defending his mentor Peel in the House of Commons itself.

After Peel's defeat over free trade in 1846, Gladstone became one of those distinguished Peelites—Sir James Graham and Edward Cardwell were two others—who were the despair of the party system. Intelligent and independent minded, they revered their fallen leader. Their talents made them highly attractive to any potential Government. Yet, as the historian G. M. Young remarked of this group of political stars, they "drifted in the political sea like an iceberg on which no man can safely land but which can easily sink a ship."

It was a period of comparative political quiescence for Gladstone, but also of distress, and much personal activity. These years marked the end of his dream of the co-operation between the Church and the State, and his concern with the increasingly Catholic direction of the religious-spiritual "rebirth" he had earlier so firmly supported. The Oxford Movement led to the reception into the Catholic Church, much to his distress, not only of its leader, John Henry Newman, but of two of Gladstone's closest friends, Henry Manning, ultimately a cardinal, and James Hope-Scott, both of whom converted in 1851. Gladstone was very sympathetic himself to High Church tendencies within the Church of England and to born Catholics like Lord Acton. But conversion to Catholicism disturbed him profoundly—he viewed it as a considerable loss to the true faith.

He was also distressed by the cruel treatment of Sir Robert Peel, who was deserted by the bulk of his party after he supported the repeal of the Corn Laws, which had in effect committed the nation to a policy of free trade.

The years 1847 to 1850 were marked for him by crushing family cares. Eventually he was able to save the Glynne family and its estate of Hawarden from the prospect of financial ruin, the consequence of an ill-judged venture into iron and steel manufacturing by his brother-in-law, Sir Stephen Glynne.

The rigorous society of his youth—rigorous in its religion, its conduct of finance, its codes of behavior—seemed to be in the process of breaking up. There was even the danger of violent revolution in 1848. Then he emphasized his own commitment to order by serving as a special constable when riot threatened London in that year of European convulsion. (In fact, the decision of the Chartists—the most powerful radical working-class movement in the first half of the nineteenth century—not to march across the Thames to confront Parliament signaled the end of effective Chartism in England.)

It was also in these years that Gladstone embarked upon his mission to attempt to rescue prostitutes from their degrading way of life, a concept that grew out of the decision of a group of his friends each to dedicate himself to some form of good works. This rescue work caused acute embarrassment to his political colleagues, the more so as he became increasingly prominent. He refused to abandon it, however, and continued to have long talks with prostitutes in the streets and in their rooms, no matter what gossip it gave rise to. One man who attempted to blackmail him Gladstone promptly turned over to the police and he was sentenced and jailed. Characteristically, Gladstone later intervened so that the man was released after having served only one quarter of his sentence. His wife fully supported him in his work, and supervised the attempt to save the fallen through placing them in special residences in London and sending some to cottages on the family estate at Hawarden. The volumes of the diaries so far published have made abundantly clear that Gladstone himself was fully aware of the complexity of his motives in his "traffic" with prostitutes. He knew that his own strong sexuality played an important part in his attraction to the rescue work; his activity intensified when his wife was away in the country preoccupied with their growing family. He told his eldest son, and spiritual adviser, Stephen, the rector of Hawarden, that he had never "betrayed the marriage bed," but the avowal seems to suggest that he had been severely tempted, despite his supremely happy marriage. Such a statement suggests a more human Gladstone than is commonly depicted; he was not the prig some believed him to be. He also had a compulsion to read pornography. When Gladstone felt his motives were too mixed in his rescue work or that he had overindulged in reading pornography he took the extreme step of punishment through self-flagellation. He indicated such action by drawing a small whip in his diary —and even here, of course, his motives, albeit unconscious, were undoubtedly mixed. It will not do to under-rate the complexity of the Victorians, and of Gladstone in particular.

In the summer of 1849 he embarked on a much-misinterpreted errand to the Continent to attempt to save the wife of one of his oldest friends, Lord Lincoln, from the penalties of adultery, but he was too late—the diaries record him lurking about hotels on Lake Como trying to run the pregnant Lady Lincoln to ground. His wife suggested they might start a home for errant peeresses (following the pattern they had established for prostitutes), presided over by Archdeacon Manning, who was still within the Anglican Church, but nothing came of that whimsical project. The note of comedy here is a reminder that in his happy personal life Gladstone had a continuing solace against the world, although he was grief-stricken at the death of his daughter Jessy in April 1850. (Her death inspired some of the most poignant passages of his diary, which was so frequently impersonal in its approach to himself and others.)

There are parallels between his private work—for the family estate, for fallen women—and his somewhat crusading attitude toward the activities of the State, especially in foreign affairs. He considered that there was a growth of vulgarity and coarseness in the conduct of English political life, exemplified in the person of Lord Palmerston, Foreign Secretary in the Government of Lord John Russell. Palmerston's single most famous moment in the Commons came at the end of a five-hour speech on June 25, 1850. He had been defending himself against a vote of censure in the House of Commons, for having sent ships to blockade Greece because she would

not pay compensation to one Don Pacifico for the looting
of his house. (Don Pacifico, a Portuguese moneylender
resident in Athens, claimed British citizenship because
he had been born in Gibraltar.) Palmerston ended his
speech—with one of the most famous sentences ever ut-
tered in the House of Commons—in a swashbuckling but
grand way: "As the Roman, in days of old, held himself
free from indignity, when he could say 'Civis Romanus
sum,' so also a British subject, in whatever land he may
be, shall feel confident that the watchful eye and the
strong arm of England will protect him against injustice
and wrong."

Two days later Gladstone delivered a reply to Palmerston. This was his first major speech on foreign policy
since he had spoken against Palmerston's aggressive policy in the Opium War of 1840, when Britain had waged
war against China to make sure she bought opium from
India. His speech of 1850 has been overshadowed by Palmerston's triumph: a moderate one in Parliament where
he had a majority of forty-six, but an overwhelming one
in the country at large, where, to the degree that it is
possible to judge public opinion, he was clearly adored.
One of the great themes of Gladstone's life was his fight
against public support for an aggressive foreign policy as
enunciated by Palmerston, and in later years by Disraeli.
Gladstone's speech represents the other tradition in British foreign policy, a more complicated one than the somewhat simpleminded "little Englandism" that was quite
frequently attributed to him.

Greece had failed to meet a series of obligations to
Britain before the Don Pacifico episode, but it served as
an excuse for Palmerston to take action—to throw Britain's weight around—to assert her position. It was against

such claims, which Gladstone considered arrogant, that he felt compelled to speak, prompted by an invincible conviction of the need for fairness. He delivered his long speech late in the evening of June 27, remarking that he would have gone into greater detail if it had not been midnight, and "at this hour, and this stage of the debate, I shall endeavour to keep the attention of the House, so far as it depends upon me, fastened only upon the principle that is involved." He felt deeply enough to reprimand some members when they talked to one another too loudly while he was reading a threatening message from Count Nesselrode, the Russian Minister of Foreign Affairs. "Are there gentlemen in this House who can pursue their idle chat, while words like these are sounding in their ears?" Serious though he was, the speech itself is not without touches of humor, as Gladstone reviewed the three cases, Don Pacifico's being the most famous, that led up to British intervention. He dwells lovingly on the extraordinary fact that a moneylender who appears to have only £30 on which to operate in the bank yet claims £30,000 for damages to his furniture; Gladstone enjoys himself speculating on the nature of the furniture, and the gullibility of the British representative in Athens and Lord Palmerston himself for accepting the claim at face value. The more serious defect, however, was that the British representatives did not, according to Gladstone, make sure that every resource of Greek law was employed before resorting to a blockade. With a nice ironic tone, he makes his point:

> As to weakness, there exists a sentiment even among some part of the political adherents of the Administration—I will not discuss or attempt to define the extent

of it, but I merely allege that it exists—a sentiment to the effect that the noble Lord [Palmerston], notwithstanding his distinguished abilities, is not altogether as prudent as he is able in the management of the foreign affairs of this country. Understand, I beg, that I am not presuming to describe what are your general sentiments; but even among a portion of those gentlemen who sit opposite, there prevails an opinion, or a suspicion, that during the times when the administration of foreign affairs is in the hands of the noble Lord, the country is too commonly apt to be near the very verge of war. . . . There are in this House a class of gentlemen professing to hold what are termed strong liberal opinions, with whom the noble Lord is in the utmost favour, because they believe that he uses energetically the influence of this country for the propagation of those opinions among other nations of the world.

Gladstone was not necessarily opposed to intervention, if, in his eyes, the cause was just. Throughout his life he was loyal to the Canningite tradition of favoring liberalism abroad. But he felt that it was necessary to discriminate between such actions and those which were products of an excess of patriotism and were chiefly important as self-aggrandizing signs of strength. He totally rejected Palmerston's claim that the British citizen as such should have a position equivalent to that of the Roman citizen of old, superior to the laws of the locality in which he happens to reside, "always, of course, with the reserve of diplomatic intervention in case those laws should palpably fail to secure for [him] results conformable to general justice." There was no justification for Britain, in this particular case, to be above the law of Greece. Gladstone thought that that law—and of course here there was disagreement—could have coped with the problem if a sufficient attempt had been made to use it. "Is it then in the case of Greece that we shall arrogate an arbitrary power to pass by and ignore the courts of law, to be our own witnesses and our own judges and jury, to decide our case and assess our own damages, and to enforce what we may choose to call our grievances by the use of military means?"

Gladstone attempted to walk a difficult tightrope, for he did not assert that Britain should abandon all those who lived abroad and were her citizens; in fact he urged that for his legal proceedings Don Pacifico should receive as much financial support as he needed. He felt that Britain must protect her rights and the rights of liberty, but not outside of the idea of a brotherhood of nations, not as a superpower. He made his points as he moved toward the conclusion of his speech:

I do not doubt he [Palmerston] has the feeling—which must, indeed, be the feeling of every Englishman, and especially of every Secretary of State in England for Foreign Affairs—which has been the feeling, I am convinced, of the various distinguished persons who have held that office since the Peace [of 1815]—of the Earl of Aberdeen, of Mr. Canning, and of the Marquess of Londonderry [Castlereagh] likewise: I mean a sincere desire that when a legitimate opportunity creates itself, and makes our duty, in conformity with the principles of public law, to exercise a British influence in the regulation of the internal affairs of other countries, that influence should be exercised in the spirit which we derive from our own free and stable form of government, and in the sense of extending to such countries, as far as they are able and desirous to receive them, institutions akin to those of which we know from experience the inestimable blessings. Upon this there can be no difference of opinion among us; no man who sits here can be the friend of absolute power any more than of license and disorder. There can be no difference upon the proposition that, considering how the nations of Europe are associated together, and, in some sense, organized as a whole, such occasions will of necessity from time to time arise; but the difference among us arises from this question: Are we, or are we not, to go abroad and make occasions for the propagation even of the political opinions which we consider to be sound? I say we are not. . . . That if in every country the name of England is to be the symbol and the nucleus of a party, the name of France, or Russia, or of Austria, may and will be the same. And are you not, then, laying the foundation of a system hostile to the real interests of freedom, and destructive to the peace of the world? . . . Interference in foreign countries, Sir, according to my mind, should be rare, deliberate, decisive in character, and effectual for its end. . . . I cannot look upon all that has taken place during the four years which are the subject-matter of this Motion, without seeing a rash desire, an habitual desire, of interference—a disposition . . . to look too slightly at the restraints imposed by the letter and spirit of the law of nations. . . . Great as is the influence and power of Britain, she cannot afford to follow, for any length of time, a self-isolating policy. It would be a contravention of the law of nature and of God, if it were possible for any single nation of Christendom to emancipate itself from the obligations which bind all other nations, and to arrogate, in the face of mankind, a position of peculiar privilege. And now I will grapple with the noble Lord on the ground which he selected for himself, in the most triumphant portion of his speech, by his reference to those emphatic words *Civis Romanus sum.* He vaunted, amidst the cheers of his supporters, that under his administration an Englishman should be, throughout the world, what the citizen of Rome had been. What then, Sir, was a Roman citizen? He was the member of a privileged caste; he belonged to a conquering race, to a nation that held all others bound down by a strong arm of power. For him there was to be an exceptional system of law; for him principles were to be asserted, and by him rights were to be enjoyed, that were denied to the rest of the world. . . . He [Palmerston] adopts in part that vain conception that we, forsooth, have a mission to be the censors of vice and folly, of abuse and imperfection, among the other countries of the world; that we are to be the universal schoolmasters; and that all those who hesitate to recognize our office can be governed only by prejudice or personal animosity, and should have the blind war of diplomacy forthwith declared against them. . . . What, Sir, ought a Foreign Secretary to be? Is he to be like some gallant knight at a tournament of old, pricking forth into the lists, armed at all points, confiding in his sinews and his skill, challenging all comers for the sake of honour, and having no other duty than to lay as many as possible of his adversaries sprawling in the dust? If such is the idea of a good Foreign Secretary, I, for one, would vote to the noble Lord his present appointment for his life. But Sir, I do not understand the duty of a Secretary for Foreign Affairs to be of such a character. I understand it to be his duty to conciliate peace with dignity. I think it to be the very first of all his duties studiously to observe, and to exalt in honour among mankind, that great code of principles which is termed the law of nations.[1]

Such were the noble principles that Gladstone set forth in his unsuccessful speech. It is particularly striking that he did not retreat into isolationism, he did not adopt the easy position that safety lay in doing nothing. He knew that it was hard to define the law of nations, but he felt that Britain had an obligation to help enforce it; she had a contrary obligation not to demand compensations and awards for herself just because she happened to be powerful.

His conception of foreign policy, set forth somewhat in the abstract in the speech on Don Pacifico, was put to a practical test through his own actions in the months following. The speech had defined his particular liberal feelings about foreign policy. His visit to Naples from October 1850 to February of the following year demonstrates the practical limits and strengths of his position. He went there because of the health of his wife and their daughter Mary. He had been aware already of the inequities in the kingdom of the Two Sicilies, and in fact in the speech of June he cited it as a case in which intervention might be justified, but in fact England should keep out: "The more we may be tempted to sympathize with Sicily, the less we admire Neapolitan institutions and usages of government, the more tenacious, as I contend, we should be of our duty to do them full justice—the more careful that we do not, because we differ from them, impair in their case the application of those great and sacred principles that govern and harmonize the intercourse between States, and from which you never can depart, without producing mischiefs by the violation of the rule, a thousand-fold greater than any benefit you may promise yourself to achieve in the special instance."

Gladstone had long been fascinated by Italy. He was there on a grand tour when he returned to contest his first parliamentary seat in 1832. As a student of the classics, as an intense admirer of Dante, fascinated with the Roman Church—anxious to bring about some sort of reconciliation with it but at the same time profoundly suspicious of its activities in England—Gladstone all through his life maintained a great affection for Italy. While there he not only collected sermons but also collected art. He regarded himself as comparatively unskilled in judging painting, but he went his own way, and had an interest in the early Italian painters, before they became fashionable, as well as in Carlo Dolci, Guido Reni, and Salvator Rosa.[2] He was a major collector until 1875. At that time he thought he was retiring for good and sold most of his collection.

He had no deep interest in the revolutions of 1848. His visit to Italy in 1850 was entirely motivated by reasons of health. But he was a political creature, and he became interested in the political activities in Naples, where Ferdinand II (King "Bomba") was busy undercutting the concessions granted in 1848. Gladstone spent much of his time visiting the courts and the prisons. He was particularly horrified at the conditions in the prisons and the brutal way in which the liberal opponents of the regime were being treated. The bad situation led him to adopt a stand of moral intervention that modified the position he had only recently taken in the Don Pacifico affair. (Ironically, the Neapolitan liberals felt that their prison conditions had been made worse because of the intervention on their behalf by the British Minister to the Kingdom of the Two Sicilies, Lord Palmerston's brother.)

Gladstone returned to England in February 1851 obsessed with the question of Italy; the experience was a crucial one in moving him in the direction of Liberalism, a growing belief that certain minimum liberties, and self-determination, belonged to all. Originally he had seen himself as a defender of order against the irrationality of the despotic government in Naples. In fact, Gladstone was advocating a crucial conservative belief, but one which served him as part of his ultimate transition to Liberalism: that the outbreak of disorder and revolution was frequently caused by excessive resistance to change, that authority is best maintained if it is combined with a certain amount of freedom. This was the principle on which both Tory and Liberal tended to agree.[3]

But when he visited the Naples of the Bourbons he found there what he considered "the negation of God erected into a system of government." He attempted through private negotiation via Lord Aberdeen, a former Foreign Secretary, to bring about some change in Naples, but he became impatient when there was no public result. In July 1851 in his famous *Two Letters to Lord Aberdeen* he attacked the regime violently for its lack of freedom and its lack of legitimate laws, and he voiced his hope that considerable pressure, short of war, could be applied in order to destroy the decadent regime. Gladstone made himself a patron saint of Italian freedom, and Palmerston was delighted that one of his chief attackers was now as intent on bringing pressure to bear upon a foreign government as he had ever been himself. Gladstone was not put off by attacks from the Austrian Foreign Secretary—attacks that Gladstone himself might have used, but did not, in doing down Palmerston: that Britain did not treat her prisoners in Ireland, in the

Ionian Islands, in Ceylon, any better than Greece may have treated Don Pacifico, or than the King of Sicily treated his prisoners. Both Palmerston and Gladstone— who was more of a Liberal upon his return from Naples than he was before—were liberal in their approach to foreign policy; both disagreed with the Metternichian tradition that the status quo and order should be maintained at practically any price. As suggested in his speech attacking Palmerston and also by his experience in Naples, Gladstone differed profoundly from Palmerston, whose primary concern was Britain's position; if the cause of better and more liberal government was served at the same time, so much the better. Gladstone's chief concern was the latter; he would not fear intervention, or at the least considerable pressure, for that purpose. He was not primarily concerned with Britain's interests, although he had no objection to the ties, financial and otherwise, that were developing between Piedmont and Britain. Also, he was rarely unaware of his own position as a politician and he had a shrewd sixth sense of how the actions he took would affect his career. He might at times seem insensitive to the nuances of politics, but that was mainly his manner; he was an astute politician. But his overwhelming concern, without being fanatic about it, was to argue for what he considered right: in the Don Pacifico affair, against sending warships to Greece; in the Two Sicilies, to marshal public pressure —he did not advocate literal intervention—to impose upon the Kingdom a better form of government. As for the latter, Palmerston, still Foreign Secretary and not adverse to liberalism even without immediate advantage, cooperated with Gladstone. Palmerston had Gladstone's inflammatory pamphlet distributed to the courts of Europe in the hope that it might help the cause of Italian liberation. Palmerston returned Gladstone's attack of the previous year with praise in the House of Commons: "Instead of seeking amusements, diving into volcanoes and exploring excavated cities, he [Gladstone] visited prisons, descended into dungeons, examined cases of the victims of illegality and injustice, and had then sought to rouse the public opinion of Europe."[4] The reception of the pamphlet in the courts of Europe was, not surprisingly, unenthusiastic, and it was not much better among those who made policy in England, those whom Gladstone would call "the Ten Thousand." In his mind, they did not want questions of morality to interfere with questions of foreign policy. In that sense, as well as in the ideas it contained, the pamphlet marked a step in Gladstone's progress toward a belief that the "people" might have better sense about foreign policy, and perhaps in other matters, than the "ruling class."

Looking back upon what had happened in Italy, when independence and unification of most of the country had come about, Gladstone was touchingly modest about his part in bringing about that conclusion. In a speech of 1862, he said: "[If] I have been in the smallest degree instrumental in assisting to cause the removal, from a world in which there is wickedness with misery and sorrow enough, of one great and gigantic iniquity [the downfall of the King of the Two Sicilies], I should accept that proof as another favour conferred upon me. I do not, however, assume to myself any credit of that character." Gladstone regarded the creation of Italy as an example of a new force in public life, which he had in fact helped bring into existence, and would use to even greater effect in the politics of the 1870's. "Moral support is a real power in Europe. Genuine public opinion—not the opinion of any one State—is a real power in Europe; and it is a true sign of advancing civilization and of progress in the affairs of men—not a visionary, but real and substantial progress—when you find that you have passed beyond the region in which no real influence was known, except that of sword clashing against sword, and entered into that domain in which the minds of men act upon one another, and in which, without a resort to force, the power of higher principles is felt and recognized."[5]

Some years earlier, one of Gladstone's most brilliant speeches on Britain's role in the world had been his attack on the British bombardment of the Canton forts in 1857. He clearly stated in the speech the need for a "moral" foreign policy. Ever since the East India Company had been replaced by the British Government as the administrating agent in India there had been serious difficulties between India and China about trade, most particularly about the opium trade, or more specifically, the Chinese reluctance to buy Indian opium. There had been war in 1840, and further difficulties in 1856, when the Chinese had boarded the *Arrow* and arrested twelve Chinese. (Although the ship was flying a British flag, and commanded by a British subject, it was owned by a Chinese from Hong Kong and was probably involved in illegitimate activities.) The *Arrow* episode led to the bombardment of the Canton forts, and there was a further series of Chinese crises that culminated in 1860—three years later—when British troops burned the Summer Palace in Peking. The final result of Western pressure was the further admission of foreign merchants to China and the legalization of the opium trade. It was hard, even if he had wished to, for Palmerston to control activities so far away—it took about six months for a round-trip communication.

Gladstone delivered a blistering attack on the bombardment, supporting a motion of censure on the incident moved by the great apostle of peace and free trade, Richard Cobden. In this particular debate Disraeli spoke on the same side as Gladstone, but in general Gladstone's sense of political independence at this time was reinforced both by his suspicion of Palmerston, now Prime Minister—a Whig with profound conservative instincts—and of Disraeli, the leading Tory in the House of Commons. The debate helped to bring down the Palmerston Government which, however, the electorate returned enthusiastically to power in the General Election that immediately followed.

Gladstone's speech emphasizes the difficulty of the role of the powerful nation. No less than his great friend the historian Lord Acton, he was keenly aware of the temptations of power. In his speech about the bombardment Gladstone raised in even clearer terms the problem that the Don Pacifico debate had represented. A State obviously has an obligation to protect its citizens at home and abroad. Yet it need not, indeed should not, in Gladstone's view, act as an agent for its merchants' financial interests. Nor should the State act on the word of those who had the most to gain. In this speech, as elsewhere, Gladstone appears to be doing penance for his own limited support of the slave trade in 1833, for in effect he criticizes himself as he was then:

> It is very well to talk of the opinions of British merchants; but it has never been the practice of Parliament, when it has been dealing with questions in

which a particular part of the community had a special and personal interest, even though that interest should be accompanied with the advantage of superior knowledge, to abdicate its own functions and to register its judgments according to the opinions of that class. I certainly . . . am one of the last men in this House who either ought to feel or could by possibility feel a disposition to throw discredit upon the class from which I am sprung; but I utterly disclaim the notion that we are to bow to this species of authority, and say it is not according to the practice of Parliament. If it had been the practice of Parliament to govern its proceedings in cases where particular classes were greatly interested by the opinions of those classes, its deliberations would have taken a very different colour from that which they now wear. We certainly, when we were considering the Factory Bills, did not take as our paramount authority the opinions of the manufacturers. When we were considering Corn Laws, we did not take as our paramount authority the opinion of the landed gentlemen. When we were considering the abolition of the slave trade we did not take as our paramount authority the voices of the Members for Liverpool; and if in 1833 the sentiments of the West India planters, with what they called their knowledge of the negro character, had been predominant, would emancipation have been given to the black population? Sir, the judgment of the merchants is an element in the case, but it does not discharge us of our responsibility to become ourselves the judges of that judgment, and to give sentence accordingly.

He was also aware of how easy it was to find excuses, incidents, to provoke the aggressive actions a powerful nation wished to take, what could be covered by "that cabalistic phrase *Insults in China.*" He felt that incidents could lead to actions that, being short of war, were no better. "No, Sir, there is not war with China, but what is there? There is hostility. There is a trampling down of the weak by the strong." He was not insensitive to the difficulties of speaking out against a policy that involves fighting, whether a full-scale war or not, and the accusations that might be made against such a stand—that the cause of humanity, of trade, upon the thinking of the Chinese themselves—all would be adversely affected if Parliament criticized British actions in China. Nonetheless, he asserted the right of the House of Commons to act and stop the undeclared war. "Every Member of the House of Commons is proudly conscious that he belongs to an assembly which in its collective capacity is the paramount power of the State."[6] Gladstone wished for a conception of "British justice and British wisdom" that would not countenance the oppression of the Chinese. He won this particular debate, and felt a slight touch of perhaps justified smugness about the 263 to 247 votes in his favor: "A division doing more honour to the House of Commons than any I ever remember."[7] But his "victory" was short-lived: Palmerston's foreign policy triumphed by the end of the decade.

Gladstone was not opposed to war as such; a war he considered to be fought for the peace of the world was acceptable to him, and so he regarded the Crimean War. But he did not approve of aggressive actions that were obviously designed to help British commercial interests or to elevate British prestige. In a way he was in part responsible for the reputation that Britain acquired of covering her aggressive actions with pious platitudes, although Palmerston himself tended to be remarkably honest. Gladstone, however, meant what he said, and he can hardly be blamed if others used his sort of language, while taking the sort of actions he had so thoroughly condemned.

FOUR

Finance

December 16, 1852; April 18, 1853;
February 10, 1860

IN 1852, GLADSTONE WAS SOMEWHAT REMOVED from the domestic political scene. He continued to concern himself with the cause of the public law of Europe in the Neapolitan case. But he was preoccupied with Manning's going over to Rome and the death of his father in December 1851. The latter event saddened him, though he felt an unreasonable resentment that he should not have been left the great family estate in Scotland. But the death of his father would, in some degree, liberate Gladstone from older financial ideas. No longer encumbered by the family tradition of an interest in the West Indies, he was noticeably hard on the West Indian sugar interests in his Budget of 1853.

Lord John Russell's Government fell in early 1852, brought down in large part by his dismissal of Palmerston after the latter approved of Louis Napoleon's coup in France. A Tory Derby–Disraeli Government was formed; Disraeli with some reluctance became Chancellor of the Exchequer. For Gladstone, 1852 was a quiet time, one in which to digest the Neapolitan experiences, and to shape in his own mind his ideas about finance, based on his being a disciple of Peel's. He felt a need for caution, but he was also freed from old economic ideas and shackles. That he was aware he was likely to be going against both family and the upper-class tradition of his upbringing is evident in a line he wrote in retrospect about this period: "The key to my position was that my opinions went one way, my lingering sympathies the other."[1] He had an early opportunity to express the sort of synthesis he was working toward—a forward-looking policy combined with a strong moral sense—in the powerful speech he gave on Disraeli's Budget.

That central Victorian pair—Gladstone and Disraeli—had the first of their many major disputes over the Budget of 1852. It would be hard to imagine two leaders more diametrically opposed. Given Disraeli's sympathy with some radical causes and Gladstone's conservative tendencies, it would not have been impossible for them both to have been in either the Tory or the Whig party. They both had that extraordinary quality necessary for a distinguished political career: a profound sense of timing and an ability to guide the House of Commons. But Gladstone, who never forgave Disraeli his hounding of Peel in the 1840's, found Disraeli morally repugnant; Disraeli thought Gladstone a hypocrite, remarking of him that he was "a sophistical rhetorician, intoxicated with the exuberance of his own verbosity, and gifted with an egotistical imagination that can at times command an interminable and inconsistent series of arguments to malign an opponent and to glorify himself."[2]

In 1852 both Disraeli and Derby recognized that their support of Protection—that is, tariffs, particularly for agriculture, which Disraeli had championed against Peel and had been the basis of his popularity—had to be abandoned, but they wished to do so as quietly as possible. They did not want to upset their followers, who had believed in 1846 that Protection was the true cornerstone of the Tory party. Through his theory of "compensation" Disraeli attempted both to accept free trade and to help those who were hurt by it, most particularly the landed, shipping, and sugar interests, through the reduction of some of the taxes they paid. The lost income was to be made up through an extension of the income tax to those of lower incomes. What was considered the unfairness of this Budget helped considerably in bringing down the Government, and one of the most telling attacks against the Government, and Disraeli, was Gladstone's speech on December 16, 1852.

The Times wrote of it that "it was pitched in a high tone of moral feeling—now rising to indignation, now sinking to remonstrance—which was sustained throughout without flagging and without effort."[3] While not stating so directly, Gladstone was able to suggest that Disraeli was a charlatan, who was presenting to Parliament a ragbag of a Budget without any guiding principle. (Although at times the personal relations of the two approached cordiality, most touchingly on the occasion of the death of Disraeli's wife in 1868, their enmity did become profound. Gladstone denied that he loathed Disraeli, but he did regard him as the grand corrupter of English public life, while Disraeli thought of Gladstone as a prig with an unrealistic conception of politics.) In his attack on the Budget, Gladstone managed to convey his moral disapproval of Disraeli sufficiently to arouse the ire of those sitting opposite, and several of his sentences were lost in cries of disapproval. The House couldn't have been livelier, even though Gladstone had risen to speak at one o'clock in the morning. He had told his wife that he found the Budget itself "disgusting and repulsive" when it was introduced on December 3, and he now was livid at the attacks that Disraeli had made on its opponents, most particularly on the Peelites. "There are some things which he [Disraeli], too, has yet to learn. . . . I must tell the right hon. gentleman that whatever he has learned—and he has learned much—he has not yet learned the limits of discretion, of moderation, and of forbearance, that ought to restrain the conduct and language of every Member of this House, the disregard of which is an offense in the meanest amongst us, but it is of tenfold weight when committed by the leader of the House of Commons." What is particularly striking about Gladstone's speech, and his later Budget, was his desire to use financial means as a way to improve the harmony of the classes, and his sensitiveness to anything that might exacerbate their relations. He objected most violently to Disraeli's way of raising money to make up for the remission of duties "which is so adroitly contrived that both of these taxes . . . shall strike precisely the same class." The money was to come from those with incomes lower than those that had previously been taxed, and from those who owned houses with lower rents. Gladstone also dwelt on the ways in which Disraeli would hurt those classes he had made so much of claiming to protect in the past, most particularly the yeoman and the clergy. It is hard to believe, whatever the goodness of Gladstone's character, that he did not derive a certain malicious pleasure from making such a point against a man who had adapted himself so readily to classes so foreign from his own urban, Jewish, literary background.

Gladstone was also outraged that some of Disraeli's Cabinet colleagues should claim that the Budget was consistent with those of Peel's. Gladstone denied this with emotion: "I may presume to have an opinion on the question of what were Sir Robert Peel's principles of commercial reform." He was particularly irked because he thought Disraeli was putting forth schemes he knew would not work, but would be attractive, in order to make a vulgar appeal to the multitude. At the same time Disraeli claimed, according to Gladstone, that his schemes would in fact hinder the development of democracy: "We are told that it is necessary to moderate and check the progress of democracy; but there is no surer way of advancing the progress of democracy than by casting loose on the world attractive and seductive schemes with regard to financial arrangements, which those who propose them know cannot be carried into effect. . . . I will ask hon. gentlemen who are so squeamish on the subject of anxiety for popularity, if they heard the speech of the right hon. Chancellor of the Exchequer, in which he has laid out before the public the good deeds of the Government, as a shopman lays out his wares. Many similar deeds have been done by former Governments, but they were never paraded before the House and country as they have been by the Chancellor of the Exchequer tonight." It was Disraeli's tone, his style, as well as the content, which so profoundly upset Gladstone's sense of what was appropriate and fair. And the lack of principle, as well as the lack of knowledge, that he felt Disraeli had shown, offended him. "It is my firm conviction that the Budget is one, I will not say the most liberal, nor the most radical, but I will say [one of] the most subversive in its tendencies and ultimate effects which I have ever known submitted to this

House. It is the most regardless of the general rules of prudence which it is absolutely necessary we should preserve, and which it is perfectly impossible that this House, as a popular assembly, should observe unless the Government sets us the examples, and uses its influence to keep up in the right course."[4]

Immediately after Gladstone's speech, Disraeli's Budget was rejected by the House of Commons at 4 A.M. by a vote of 305 to 286. In the Government that Lord Aberdeen formed in succession, the Peelites cooperated and Gladstone became Chancellor of the Exchequer. He and Disraeli had an unseemly private dispute about the transfer of the furniture and official Chancellor's robes in 11 Downing Street, the residence of the Chancellor of the Exchequer (Disraeli kept the robes).

On April 18, 1853, Gladstone delivered in four and three-quarters hours his first Budget. He attempted to introduce, in some degree, a free-trade economy, consistent with his earlier work on the Board of Trade. At the same time the Budget was one of his first gestures toward the great majority of taxpayers and away from "the Ten Thousand." He subjected real as well as personal property to a legacy tax, a significant blow against land. Land in the eyes of the gentlemen of England always had a special right to be treated much more reverently than any other form of property. Gladstone did not hesitate to intrude himself into the various sanctums of privilege. He wished to eliminate as best he could any unfairnesses in taxation. The speech demonstrated an extraordinary fluency, ranging from the most detailed command of figures to the consideration of principles. He could be severe, as when denying that anything could be done for the West Indian sugar interests: "It is entirely impossible for the Government to hold out the smallest hope." And as part of his facing necessities, he went into a long disquisition on the income tax, which had been introduced by Pitt. It was extremely unpopular, and Gladstone himself disliked it because he felt that it was conducive to fraud, "involving, as it necessarily does, to so large an extent, the objectionable principle of self-assessment. . . . [It encouraged] the tendency to immorality, which is I fear, essentially inherent in the nature of the operation." He also objected to the inquisitions it entailed and invasions of privacy. He went into a lengthy discussion of how the income tax worked, and of his hope to effect its eventual elimination by 1860. The income tax did not end then, and has not ended since, but Gladstone's wish demonstrates his willingness and desire to plan over a long range: "This country . . . cannot bear a reconstruction of the income tax once a year." But while it lasted he felt that it should be fair; that the balance of the income tax between what was paid by land on the one hand and trade on the other was not equitable. There should be, he felt, a better balance between the taxes paid by intelligence and skill and those paid by property. "What we understand to be the sentiment of the country, and what we ourselves, as a matter of feeling, are disposed to defer to, and to share in, is, that the income tax bears upon the whole too hard upon intelligence and skill, and not hard enough upon property as compared with intelligence and skill." That might be a sentiment in the country, but it was not a dominant one in the House of Commons, nor was it the feeling in the Cabinet until Gladstone had worked long and hard upon them—as he would do in the House as well. Gladstone felt that the financial stipulations must not discriminate in favor of one class. His careful proposals about the ways of using the income tax had their object, not achieved then or later, that "on the 5th of April, 1860, the income tax will expire." Also, on the behalf of fairness, he introduced a legacy duty in order to force property to pay more than it had in the past. He felt that with a payment upon death "the liability to pay occurs only within the limitation which the laws of a higher Power have ordained; that it only occurs once, on the death of a man; and that no man can die more than once." He felt that a legacy tax would eliminate "the greatest mischief of taxes upon property [which] is the liability of a constant recurrence of those struggles of classes which are often associated with them."

The continuation of the income tax and the imposition of a legacy tax were the difficult parts of the Budget. The remission of duties was its pleasant part, which helped provide the better life of England in the 1850's. He introduced that section of the Budget with a comparatively lyrical passage, a contrast to the extraordinarily detailed account and discussion contained in most of the speech: "As I have done with that most offensive part of my task, the imposition of taxation, I feel as it is said men are wont to feel—and as some of us have felt—when they have ended their long upward journey and reached at length the summit of the Alps. Now I have the downward road before me and the plains of Italy are in my view. I come then, Sir, to consider the more agreeable subject of the remission of taxation."

The decrease in taxes was almost completely in the direction of free trade, cutting down the duties paid on goods and foods coming into England. The duties were not completely removed, but that was the potential outcome. He also reduced stamp duties, which would be completely taken off newspapers by June 1855. The growth of the popular press would mean much to the size of the audience that politicians, and Gladstone in particular, would reach in the years to come. He also decreased the taxes paid on servants, private carriages, and horses, but he increased the taxes paid on dogs! He did not reduce the duty on wine, and gave little hope there, in a bleak statement: "While we cannot propose any change in it at the present time, neither can we see any definite or early prospect of a change hereafter." He did, however, reduce the duty on tea, and on approximately 130 other foods, among them apples, cheese, cocoa, nuts, eggs, oranges and lemons, butter, and raisins. Ordinary life was clearly going to become somewhat cheaper. Gladstone said in conclusion to this section of his speech "that while we have sought to do justice, by the changes we propose in taxation, to intelligence and skill, as compared with property—while we have sought to do justice to the great labouring community of England by further extending their relief from indirect taxation, we have not been guided by any desire to put one class against another . . . by adapting it to ourselves as a sacred aim, to diffuse and distribute—burden if we must; benefit if we may—with equal and impartial hand."

Of course he did not achieve some of his objectives, most particularly the elimination of the income tax. He believed in financing the Crimean War of 1854–1856 by doubling taxation to 1s. 2d. in the pound rather than an increase in the debt. And his expectations from the legacy tax were disappointed. But it was a Budget that attempted to operate along a set of principles of equalizing the burden of taxation and of increasing the scope of free trade. It moved in a direction to make life better for the newer classes in British society, to give greater substance to the victories won by the Reform Act of 1832, which had expanded the franchise, and by the repeal of the Corn Laws in 1846, whereby the principle of free trade was established. The further elimination of duties —in the classical liberal pattern of not taking positive steps, but of removing restrictions—made a pleasanter life available to more British men and women. Gladstone was raised in the world of Britain before Reform and accepted many of its values, yet he was deeply concerned with the need to be fair, to treat citizens equally. He was slowly moving toward a belief in a freer, slightly more egalitarian society. His genuine hopes were to be found in the rather traditional hyperbole with which he ended his first Budget speech: "We have the consolation of believing that by proposals such as these we contribute, as far as in us lies, not only to develop the material resources of the country, but to knit the hearts of the various classes of this great nation yet more closely than heretofore to that Throne and to those institutions under which it is their happiness to live."[5]

The 1850's were a period of flux for British politics, as they were for Gladstone, a time for regrouping and reconsideration, and for the shaping of the Conservative and Liberal parties as they were to function at least until 1886. He was Chancellor of the Exchequer in Aberdeen's Government, a mixture of Whigs and Peelites, in which the latter dominated. Aberdeen would have been a fine peace Minister but he was saddled with the Crimean War, the most serious war of those Britain fought between 1815 and 1914, with the possible exception of the

Boer War at the end of the century. Contrary to his later position over the Eastern Question, Gladstone strongly supported the Government's anti-Russian policy and what he regarded as a legitimate curtailment of Russia's expansionist intentions.

Aberdeen resigned in 1855, when he lost the vote on Roebuck's motion calling for a committee of inquiry into the conduct of the Crimean War—a direct challenge to his leadership. Gladstone hoped that a Cabinet would be formed similar to the one just dissolved. Palmerston, who had been Foreign Secretary under Aberdeen until 1853, formed a Government at the Queen's request—she had no choice but to ask him to do so. Three leading Peelites— Graham, Herbert, and Gladstone—joined for two weeks. But they found they were unwilling to associate with Palmerston as leader, and were unhappy about the Committee of Inquiry. Gladstone wrote long afterward, in 1897, about this moment, revealing his own later awareness of the slowness with which he had moved toward a firm affiliation with Liberalism: "I think that though perfectly satisfied to be in a Peelite government which had whigs or radicals in it, I was not ready to be in a whig government which had Peelites in it. It took a long time, with my slow-moving and tenacious character, for the Ethiopian to change his skin."[6] Perhaps his real allegiance lay with the official Conservative party. He could join the Earl of Derby, its leader. In 1857 Gladstone and Disraeli, Derby's lieutenant, had a rare moment of cooperation as foes of increased expenditure. Gladstone might completely go over to the Tory side, particularly as he was finding Palmerstonian foreign policy more and more distasteful. But at the end of 1858 he removed himself from the picture by leaving England—on behalf of the new brief ministry formed by the Tory Lord Derby—to be Lord High Commissioner Extraordinary for the Ionian Islands, which had been ruled by the British since 1815 but yearned to be part of Greece. As a passionate Panhellenist, a distinguished if very idiosyncratic Homeric scholar, Gladstone was delighted with the post. He tried to steer a middle course, and naturally satisfied no one. He failed to find a solution and a few years later the islands became part of Greece. The exotic experience intensified his sense of the difficulties of nationalism, the obligations of an occupying power, and the problem of reconciling freedom with rational arrangements. But it did not lessen his sympathy for an oppressed people: his trip back to England through Italy—including a meeting with Cavour—increased his fervor for the Italian cause. Italy provided an important reason, as well as a cover, for Gladstone's rejoining Palmerston. Over that country, the two sorts of liberal foreign policy, basically so different, could coalesce. Gladstone moved slowly and reluctantly. Although he voted in favor of the Derby Government when it lost the motion of confidence that ended its ministry on June 10, 1859, he did not see himself as a follower of Derby, who was less sympathetic than the Whig-Liberals to the war for Italian unification presently being waged. But would Gladstone join Palmerston, who wanted him for his speaking abilities, his ideas, and his financial skill? Palmerston had already managed to make up his quarrel with Lord John Russell, the former Prime Minister, and so could attract the Whigs, the Radicals, and he hoped other Peelites. At length, Gladstone consented to enter the new Government as Chancellor of the Exchequer. This could be regarded as the final step in the reconstruction of a party system that had been destroyed in 1846, the coming together of various factions that might just be considered on the left of the political spectrum, symbolized by a meeting on June 6 where Palmerston, Russell, and John Bright spoke. The cause of Italy and Gladstone's detestation of Disraeli had made him into a Liberal. But his whole cast of mind and the general direction of his thought had predisposed him, in fact, to be more inclined toward Liberal thought— even though in many social and religious questions he still had strong residual sympathies with the Tories.

Gladstone had altruistic motives concerning what he considered "public right" in foreign policy. As he wrote to an Italian friend, his main reason for going into the Government was to help Italy "and of the important though I hope pacific part which England may have to play in bringing it to a happy settlement."[7] But the long-range effect of Gladstone's action was not limited to Italy —the immediate fight over events there much more concerned Palmerston and Russell, their disagreements with the Queen, and the various aggressive steps taken by Napoleon III. But Gladstone was crucial in keeping Palmerston and Britain firmly but pacifically supporters of Italian unification.

Palmerston recognized that Gladstone was the Liberal leader of the future. As he remarked some years later, "Gladstone will soon have it all his own way and whenever he gets my place we shall have strange doings."[8]

There was to be a Gladstonian Liberal party, in which Gladstone would attempt to infuse the principles he had developed since 1833, and was still in the process of developing. As for finance and trade, in which he had played such a significant part in 1852 and 1853, he would make his most immediate contribution by putting through Parliament the commercial treaty that Richard Cobden, the great free trader, had negotiated with Napoleon III. The treaty was an important step in completing the achievement of free trade, and in presenting the treaty and the Budget in February 1860, Gladstone had to reassure both those who were worried about the loss of revenue that would result from the lowering or the elimination of duties, and those who objected in chauvinistic terms to making any sort of arrangement with France, the traditional enemy. Gladstone succeeded so well on the latter count that he caused trouble in France: some Frenchmen thought that if the treaty was so beneficial to Britain it must be harmful to their country. Gladstone did not regard the treaty as a bargain, but rather as an arrangement of great value to both countries. It was an international move to supplement the free-trade direction he had indicated in 1852 and 1853.

He also had to defend the treaty against those pure free traders who believed that a commercial treaty by definition was a conspiracy in restraint of trade. To them Gladstone said on February 10, 1860: "We, however, have no exclusive engagements; we have not the pretence of an exclusive engagement. France is perfectly aware that our legislation makes no distinction between one nation and another, and that what we enact for her we shall at the same time enact for all the world. . . . This treaty is an abandonment of the principle of protection. . . . The fact is, and you will presently see that it is so, that our old Friend Protection, who used formerly to dwell in the palaces of the land, and who was dislodged from them some ten or fifteen years ago, has since that period found very comfortable shelter and good living in holes and corners; and you are now invited, if you will have the goodness to concur in the operation, to see whether you cannot likewise eject him from those holes and corners."

The treaty, to begin with, was a further triumph for the manufacturing interests. According to the treaty, France agreed to eliminate or reduce her duties on coal, coke, iron, steel, tools, machinery, yarns, hemp, jute, glass, stoneware, earthenware, and porcelain. In return, England would eliminate duties not just for France, but for all countries. "England engages, with a limited power of exception, which we proposed to exercise with respect only to two or three articles, to abolish immediately and totally all duties upon all manufactured goods. There will be a clean sweep, clean, entire, and absolute, of manufactured goods from the face of the British tariff." Of course, Britain was way ahead as a manufacturing power, but Gladstone did not make this engagement as a matter of calculation, but rather as a matter of principle. He believed in free trade, and he also firmly believed that free trade was a way to improve the lot of the poorer classes. He argued persuasively that duties profoundly affect the life of all but the rich. Luxury items will enter a country no matter what the duty, and the duty was a much smaller proportion of, say, an expensive pair of gloves than of a cheaper pair. Therefore, those who might be able to afford the better foreign product if there were no duty or little duty, are forced to buy protected, shoddy native goods. It is striking how frequently Gladstone saw the various economic steps that he campaigned for as helping the lot of all in England, and also as ways of lessening class antagonisms.

There would, it is true, be a loss of revenue with the duties abolished, and Gladstone went into particulars—

but as he pointed out, the loss in revenue would also mean considerable relief to the consumer, who would save, according to his calculations, £1,737,000; he estimated that the revenue loss would be £1,190,000. The consumer then would be freer to make his own decisions on how to spend his money. Before 1860, but after the various inroads made upon duties by previous Peelite and Gladstonian actions, there had been 419 commodities still subject to duty. Gladstone now successfully cut the number down to 48.[9] From the deputations he had received, he also knew that British manufacturers were extremely interested in the abolition, or at least the reduction, of duties on goods entering foreign countries, but not at all enthusiastic about reciprocal arrangements. As Gladstone said, the manufacturers, not surprisingly, demonstrated feelings, despite their denials, very similar to those of the landed classes when the repeal of the Corn Laws was discussed. "In fact, there is generally, on the part of the most respectable classes, a desire for the protection of their own business. They show that though they are without exception adherents of free trade, they are not adherents of free trade without exception."

The treaty also reduced the duty paid by brandy and wine. Gladstone demonstrated the distance that separated him from the Nonconformist teetotaler by his almost ardent section on the advantage of lowering the duty on wine. He was aware of the argument that the English were not wine drinkers, but he maintained that they had once been so, and could be so again. "You find a great number of people in this country who believe, like an article of Christian faith, that an Englishman is not born to drink French wines. . . . What they maintain is absolutely the reverse of the truth, for nothing is more certain than the taste of English people at one time for French wine. . . . I have seen it stated, and have no reason to doubt the assertion, that in 1687 there were imported into this country 3,800,000 gallons of French wine, or nearly two-thirds of the whole quantity of foreign wine which we now consume." Gladstone was well aware of how considerations shape the habits of a people, and make them appear as permanent proclivities. "Wine is the rich man's luxury, and you may make tea, or sugar, or any other article of consumption, the rich man's luxury if you put on it sufficient weight of duty. By that means you will not only effectually bar the access of the poor man to it, but will reserve to yourselves the proud satisfaction of saying with literal truth, 'Our indirect taxes are paid by the rich; none are levied upon articles consumed by the poor.' " Except for the rich, the duties imposed resulted not in protection but in prohibition of consumption. Gladstone did not feel that it would be a serious loss if British wines, and even colonial wines, were forced out of the market, despite the efforts made to popularize them. "We have heard of Cape wine, and if we visit places much frequented by what may be termed the lower middle classes we see advertisements representing large tuns surrounded by jovial people, with the words Cape port and African sherry written on them." His final touching argument was on behalf of health:

Now, I make my appeal to the friends of the poor man. There is a time which comes to all of us—the time, I mean, of sickness—when wine becomes a common necessary. What kind of wine is administered to the poor man in this country? We have got a law which makes it impossible for the poor man when he is sick to obtain the comfort and support derived from good wine, unless he is fortunate enough to live in the immediate neighbourhood of some rich and charitable friend. Consult the medical profession; ask what sort of wine is supplied to boards of guardians in this country; go on board the Queen's ships, and see the wine supplied there. Some time ago I had the honour of being on board Her Majesty's ship *Scourge,* at a time when an accident had happened to one of the sailors. I went to see the man when he was recovering from the effects of an operation. "What wine do you give him?" I asked. "We give him the wine of our mess," the surgeon told me; "we cannot give him the wine supplied to the ship." He moreover insisted on my drinking some of the ship wine, and certainly it was with great difficulty I succeeded in accomplishing the operation.

Who could resist such arguments, when Gladstone concluded after this touching story: "I believe I have now gone through the principal heads of the Commercial Treaty with France. I do not think that the friends of free trade, or those who are anxious respecting the revenue, will find fault with the provisions of the treaty."[10]

It is not surprising, given his belief in the dissemination of the written word, that he should have added to this speech a section proposing a reduction of paper duties. Complementing the removal of the stamp tax on newspapers, it was intended to make the commodity of knowledge more available (because less expensive) to more and more people. But the provision was defeated by the House of Lords—covertly supported by the Prime Minister, Palmerston—and their action led Gladstone to take one of his earliest steps to circumvent that House.

Financial and budgetary provisions had gone as separate Bills to the House of Lords, which traditionally did not interfere with them. But it was not too difficult for the Lords to destroy a particular Bill with the claim that it was not primarily a financial measure. In his next Budget —that of 1861—Gladstone introduced the practice of sending the Budget up to the House of Lords as one omnibus Bill. It was a shrewd tactical move: thereafter, the House of Lords would not find the courage to reject a Budget for almost fifty years.

The three speeches considered here—the attack on Disraeli's Budget in 1852, the presentation of the Budget of 1853, and the commercial treaty and Budget speech of 1860—reflect an unwavering dedication on Gladstone's part to his belief in fairness for all classes, removing restrictions that would not allow all classes to choose, at the lowest possible economic cost, what they might wish to buy, how they might wish to live. There should be no favoritism, neither toward those who derived income from land nor toward those who manufactured goods threatened by foreign competition.

In the period of prosperity of the 1850's it had seemed to him that the economic steps he proposed would be sufficient to make England a good society. In the 1860's, now that he was firmly within the Liberal party (on March 30, 1860, he took the symbolic step of resigning from the great Conservative club, the Carlton), he would discover that there were areas where political reform was still necessary before the sort of England he wished to see could come into being.

Apart from their detailed provisions, his speeches on finance made clear his principles of economics. They were simple enough: he believed in the removal of restrictions and the practice of thrift. Thanks to Gladstone, the presentation of the Budget became the most dramatic moment in the parliamentary year, and he could make the practice of economy exciting both to Parliament and the public, no mean feat. He led the way to what would become the great Liberal doctrine of "Peace, Retrenchment, and Reform." As doctrine, it tended in the working out to elude precise definition. In a general sort of way, however, it resisted action and control by the State in favor of a State which "held the ring" and would enable the individual to reach his full potentiality.

Gladstone, in addition, saw his economic policies as an alternative to burdensome, and costly, warlike preparations; the commercial treaty with France was a specific alternative to the expensive fortifications scheme proposed by Palmerston. Where economy was concerned, no aspect was too small for him: "The chancellor of the exchequer should boldly uphold economy in detail; and it is the mark of a chicken-hearted chancellor when he shrinks from upholding economy in detail, when because it is a question of only two or three thousand pounds, he says is no matter. He is ridiculed, no doubt, for what is called candle-ends and cheese-parings, but he is not worth his salt if he is not ready to save what are meant by candle-ends and cheese-parings in the cause of the country."[11] In his subsequent financial career he carried his principles into practice. This Budget of 1860 marked the great triumph of free trade; his further Budgets would be notable for the reduction of expenditures, a dramatic contrast to those of the rest of the century. Thus, in the period from 1860 to 1866, when he was Chancellor of the Exchequer, the overall Budget was marked by a decrease of 7 percent. From 1868 to 1873, when Robert Lowe was

Chancellor and Gladstone Prime Minister, the overall Budget went down 6 percent. It was true that when he was Chancellor of the Exchequer and Prime Minister in the first two years of his second ministry, from 1880 to 1882, there was a 7 percent rise in the Budget on domestic expenses; in those years, however, both army and naval spending was reduced, and the rise was much less than during Tory governments before and after. Gladstone maintained the same low increase of expenditure in the next three years of his government, when H. C. E. Childers was Chancellor. Even though military spending in those years went up to a considerable extent, the overall Budget only increased by 3 percent.[12] Skeptical of "growth," Gladstone was a distinctly unmodern figure in his determination that government should spend less. Yet it has to be said that such an attitude looks less old-fashioned to us in the 1970's than it might have some years ago.

FIVE

Reform

May 11, 1864; April 27, 1866

THE PERIOD OF THE EARLY 1860's was a time of consoli-
dation for Gladstone, almost as if he were waiting pa-
tiently for his inheritance. It was also a time of fruition
for his financial policy. In Morley's words he "raised
finance to the high place that belonged to it in the interest, curiosity, and imperious concern of every sound
self-governing community. Even its narrowest technicali-
ties by his supple and resplendent power as orator were
suffused with life and colour."[1] He still had to guard
himself against his inability to see the implications of his
sometimes sweeping statements; and he was still likely to
allow the aristocratic prejudices that he had acquired in
his youth to lead him astray. On October 7, 1862, at Newcastle, he ruffled the feelings of many Liberals and Radicals by suggesting that Jefferson Davis was about to succeed in creating a nation out of the Confederacy. "There
is no doubt that Jefferson Davis and other leaders of the
South have made what is more than either [an army or
navy], they have made a nation." Such a statement would
be taken to imply, quite wrongly but reasonably, that the

British Government was about to recognize the South as a separate nation. It should be remembered that this speech was made before Lincoln had pledged himself to emancipation. At the time in Britain only Radicals like John Bright saw the primary issue in the Civil War as slavery. At this moment of Southern triumph, Gladstone favored a peace through Anglo-French mediation that would recognize the division of the Union. (He and his wife were doing their best for the Lancashire workers thrown out of work by the cotton famine, employing them to make paths on the Hawarden estate and feeding there a thousand a day that autumn.) Years later he saw the statement as "not only a mistake but one of incredible grossness." It was on this very visit to Newcastle that he sensed his popularity with the multitude. He was seen as their defender, particularly on the issue of taxes on paper. Also, the great shipbuilders of Newcastle and their employees might not have reacted adversely to such a statement about the South since they saw the North as a major manufacturing rival. For whatever reasons, Gladstone proceeded down the River Tyne as if he were on a royal progress.

During these years he was also slowly moving toward a belief that there should be an increase in the franchise. This he revealed to the somewhat startled world on May 11, 1864. There had been outside of Parliament increasing agitation for a further extension of the franchise, accentuated by the formation of Reform organizations, demonstrations of support for the rebels in Poland, and most excitingly an outpouring of enthusiasm when Garibaldi visited London in April 1864. When a Private Member's Bill—that is, one not sponsored by the Government—came before Parliament, proposing an increase in the number of British who should be entitled by law to the vote, Gladstone chose to speak on it. Palmerston had been at pains to warn him that he was not to commit the Government to any particular sum a taxpayer was to pay which would give him a vote in a borough. Gladstone followed his leader's instructions literally, stating that whether or not there should be a reduction from a £10 to a £6 franchise: "in a state of opinion such as now subsists, it would not be advisable, I might even say it would not be justifiable, for the Government of the Queen, however it might be composed, to submit a measure on this subject to Parliament." But he did far exceed Palmerston's expectations in the whole spirit of his speech. The Prime Minister was clearly no friend to a further extension of the vote to any members of the working class. As he wrote to Gladstone the very day of the speech, but before it was given, "No doubt many working men are as fit to vote as many of the Ten Pounders, but if we open the door to the Class the number who may come in may be excessive, and may swamp the Classes above them. This result would arise not merely from the number let in, but also from the fact that the influx discourages the Classes above them for voting at all; and then these working men are unfortunately under the control of Trades Unions, which unions are directed by a small number of directing agitators." It might be said that it was a statement at the end of Palmerston's letter —on the questionable nature of the working class—that Gladstone was particularly concerned with refuting in his speech.

The speech began as one of his more confusing and equivocal—as if he thought it better not to be too clear and so to be able to state what he wished without offend-

ing members of his own party. But as the speech proceeded, and he warmed to his task, his meaning became
clearer. He began by stating the obvious, that the Tory
Opposition felt the franchise should stay as it was, and
that opinions were divided on the Liberal side of the
House. Although he said that nothing was to be done
about the franchise at this moment, he then went on to
say that something should be done soon, as the interplay
between debate in Parliament and public opinion was,
he believed, bringing the issue to fruition. Indeed, the
issue of the franchise was part of his idea that "ripeness
is all"—that at the right moment the correct step would
be taken—and he appeared to feel that the moment was
approaching: "Yet I am convinced that the discussion of
the question in the House of Commons must, through
the gentle process by which Parliamentary debates act
on the public mind, gradually help to bring home the
conviction that we have not been so keenly alive to our
duties in this matter as we ought to have been; that it is
for the interests of the country that this matter should
be entertained; and that it ought, if we are wise, to be
brought to an early settlement. The conditions requisite
for dealing with it can only be supplied by a favourable
state of the public mind; but the public mind is itself
guided, and opinion modified, in no small degree, by the
debates of Parliment."

Gladstone certainly agreed to the principle of an extension of the franchise, within limits. "There ought to
be, not a wholesale, nor an excessive, but a sensible and
considerable addition to that portion of the working
classes—at present almost infinitesimal—which is in pos-
session of the franchise." He completely rejected the idea
that any change would mean, as the opponents of Reform

suggested, revolution. "Is there no choice between ex-
cluding forty-nine out of every fifty working men on the
one hand, and on the other a 'domestic revolution'?" In
support for the need for change, Gladstone brought forward his conception of the nature of the workingman,
and how he should act. As he was to demonstrate later
over the question of Ireland, he attempted to avoid the
dilemma that has so frequently marked British handling
of potentially discontented groups: if there is quiet, it
is not necessary to do anything; if there is protest, it is
a sign of weakness to give in to it. Citing the argument
that there was no need to extend the franchise since there
had been no agitation from those who might gain the
vote, he asked: "Is it desirable that we should wait until
they do agitate? In my opinion, agitation by the working
classes, upon any political subject whatever, is a thing not
to be waited for, not to be made a condition previous to
any Parliamentary movement; but, on the contrary, it is
a thing to be deprecated, and, if possible, anticipated and
prevented by wise and provident measures." He told a
personal morality tale of a deputation of London workingmen, representing a large union, that called upon him
about an Annuity Bill. The deputation went on to say
that there was dissatisfaction about the franchise. Gladstone replied that the parliamentary situation was in part
in reaction to the "inaction, and alleged indifference, of
the working classes themselves." The leaders of the deputation said, and it made a deep impression upon him: "It
is true that, since the abolition of the Corn Laws, we have
given up political agitation; we have begun from that
time to feel that we might place confidence in Parliament; that we might look to Parliament to pass beneficial
measures without agitation. We were told then to aban-

don those habits of political action which had so much interfered with the ordinary occupations of our lives; and we have endeavoured to substitute for them the employment of our evenings in the improvement of our minds."

Gladstone's sense of fairness, and his belief in the need for keeping the peace, made him feel that such a commendable attitude deserved a reward. He did not agree that since the working classes (and it is notable that he almost always refers to classes in the plural) were quiet, nothing need be done. Inaction might drive them to agitation. Unlike other classes they had far less leisure time available in which to apply political pressure; hence frequently they had no choice but to demonstrate, which can easily lead to violence. Gladstone certainly did not visualize anything approaching a total enfranchisement of the working class, and there was never any question in his mind of giving votes to women. For him any measure that would raise the proportion of working-class voters in a particular constituency to two thirds of the vote would be dangerous. Approximately one third would, he believed, be a sensible quota, and would avoid the creation of a considerable working-class interest.

Gladstone rejected thinking in class or group terms. But if he believed that the worker must individually deal with his employer, he did recognize the disadvantages under which the working classes labored. He had the compassion to see that Benthamite doctrine made better sense in theory than in the case of a particular worker:

> Let us take, too, that which in former times I believe to have been the besetting sin of labour—the disposition of the majority not to recognize the right of the minority, and indeed, of every single individual, to

sell his labour for what he thinks fit. On behalf of the labouring classes, I must, in passing, say that this doctrine is much harder for them to practice than for us to preach. In our condition of life and feeling, we have nothing analogous to that which the working man cannot but feel when he sees his labour being, as he thinks, undersold. Yet still it is our duty to assert in the most rigid terms, and to carry high the doctrine of the right of every labouring man, whether with or against the approval of his class, to sell his labour as high or as low as he pleases.

Gradually he developed an argument that the working classes had acquired the right for some of them to be enfranchised. First, though, he dwelt on the class antagonism which had characterized the years since 1815: certain ideas circulated that were not in the "spirit of the old British Constitution" but rather reflected the "lamentable excesses of the first French Revolution." The misfortune of these ideas, to Gladstone's mind, was that they propagated the notion to both the lower and the ruling classes that antagonism between them was inevitable. The Government, in its employment of spies and its attack on habeas corpus, had helped to bolster such feelings. But now, he asserted, the workingman had "confidence in the law, in Parliament, and even in the executive Government."

Following this remark Gladstone committed one of his few infelicities of speech, or an ambiguity that he did not intend: "Of this gratifying state of things it fell to my lot to receive a single, indeed, but a significant proof no later than yesterday." The opposition took this to mean that this admirable state of affairs was premised on one in-

stance that had just happened, and reacted with *"cries of*
'No, no!' *and laughter!"* to which Gladstone replied,
"The quick-witted character of hon. Gentlemen opposite
outstrips, I am afraid, the tardy movement of my observations." The event to which Gladstone referred was a
deputation from the Society of Amalgamated Engineers,
who wished to invest a large part of their funds in the
State through the Post Office savings bank. Gladstone was
aware that the State could easily appear as an agent of
the ruling class. A belief by the working classes that this
was not so, that it was not necessary to keep a "jealous
independence of all direct relations with the Government," was the requisite step before there could be an
extension of the franchise. Worthiness should come before the award is given.

Gladstone did not have a social program, but he felt
that economic measures found in his Budgets had increased the liberty of the working classes, had provided
a better life, and were a means of social improvement.
And he had reason to believe that at least some of the
working classes agreed with him. Gladstone was probably
correct in his belief that the working classes were better
off in the 1860's than they were before, and that they had
greater possibilities for improving themselves. He quoted
a resolution moved at a meeting in the Potteries, although he gives no indication of the occasion: "The great
measures that have been passed during the last twenty
years by the British Legislature have conferred incal-
culable blessings on the whole community, and particularly on the working classes, by unfettering the trade and
commerce of the country, cheapening the essentials of
our daily sustenance, placing a large proportion of the

comforts and luxuries of life within our reach, and rendering the obtainment of knowledge comparatively easy among the great mass of the sons of toil."

The second part of the workers' resolution, which looked to the future, had an interesting, if perhaps uneasy, combination of deference and a sense of a need for change. "Pardon us for alluding to the kindly conduct now so commonly evinced by the wealthier portions of the community to assist in the physical and moral improvement of the working classes. The well-being of the toiling mass is now generally admitted to be an essential to the national weal. This forms a pleasing contrast to the opinions cherished half a century ago. The humbler classes also are duly mindful of the happy change, and, without any abatement of manly independence, fully appreciate the benefits resulting therefrom, contentedly fostering a hopeful expectation of the future."

Gladstone then went on to the most famous part of the speech: that the franchise should be open to those who are worthy. In the context of the paragraph itself, as well as within the context of the speech, which did not advocate any immediate action and was definitely not in favor of any total enfranchisement, the statement about "the pale of the Constitution" was qualified and limited. But for many, notably the Tories, the Queen and Palmerston on one side, and the working classes on the other, Gladstone was taken as having promised a vast step forward on the path to democracy. He had been most impressed by those Lancashire workingmen who had faced the cotton famine of 1862 and who nevertheless had supported the North in the American Civil War. Gladstone in fact exaggerated the extent to which the cotton workers had acted contrary to their economic interests:

And I venture to say that every man who is not pre-sumably incapacitated by some consideration of per-sonal unfitness or of political danger is morally entitled to come within the pale of the Constitution. Of course, in giving utterance to such a proposition, I do not recede from the protest I have previously made against sudden, or violent, or excessive, or intoxicating change; but I apply it with confidence to this effect, that fitness for the franchise, when it is shown to exist—as I say it is shown to exist in the case of a select portion of the working class—is not repelled on sufficient grounds from the portals of the Constitution by the allegation that things are well as they are. I contend, moreover, that persons who have prompted the expression of such sentiments as those to which I have referred, and whom I know to have been members of the working class, are to be presumed worthy and fit to discharge the duties of citizenship, and that to admission to the discharge of those duties they are well and justly entitled. The present franchise, I may add, on the whole—subject, of course, to some exceptions—draws the line between the lower middle class and the upper order of the working class. As a general rule, the lower stratum of the middle class is admitted to the exercise of the franchise, while the upper stratum of the working class is excluded. That I believe to be a fair general description of the present formation of the constituencies in boroughs and towns. Is it a state of things, I would ask, recom-mended by clear principles of reason? Is the upper portion of the working classes inferior to the lowest portion of the middle? That is a question I should wish to be considered on both sides of the House. For my own part, it appears to me that the negative of the proposition may be held with the greatest confidence. Whenever this Question comes to be discussed, with the view to an immediate issue, the conduct of the general body of the operatives of Lancashire cannot be forgotten. What are the qualities which fit a man for the exercise of a privilege such as the franchise? Self-command, self-control, respect for order, patience under suffering, confidence in the law, regard for superiors; and when, I should like to ask, were all these great qualities exhibited in a manner more signal, I would even say more illustrious, than under the profound affliction of the winter of 1862? I admit the danger of dealing with enormous masses of men; but I am now speaking only of a limited portion of the working class, and I, for one, cannot admit that there is that special virtue in the nature of the middle class which ought to lead to our drawing a marked distinction, a distinction almost purporting to be one of principle, between them and a select portion of the working classes, so far as relates to the exercise of the franchise.

This was the high moment of the speech, and it was difficult not to regard Gladstone's statement as a firm commitment to expand the franchise. The speech was an important contribution to his growing popularity in the country. The premise of his approach was that the franchise was not a right—that every man by definition is entitled to the vote—but rather, a privilege. To participate in the State is an honor to which a claim, of property, of interest, or worthiness, must first be tendered, before the gates to the Constitution are opened. What startled Gladstone's hearers was his contention that the premises on which admission would be granted would be expanded to include more and more voters, as more and more members of the community would demonstrate that they possessed these qualities. As though he had forgotten Palmerston's injunction, he suggested there should not be too long a delay before some extension of the franchise be granted: "I, for myself, confess that I think the investigation will be far better conducted if we approach the question at an early date, in a calm frame of mind, and without having our doors besieged by crowds, or our table loaded with petitions; rather than if we postpone entering upon it until a great agitation has arisen." Since he saw the franchise as a favor to be granted from above, he wished Parliament to act in accord with that premise before they were forced to grant the vote without receiving any gratitude from those who were enfranchised. "Hearts should be bound together by a reasonable extension, at fitting times, and among selected portions of people, of every benefit and every privilege that can justly be conferred upon them."[2]

Gladstone had some reason to think that he had been moderately clear in his speech about his hopes and their limitations. Consciously or not, he must have realized that in politics ideas are often simplified and vulgarized so that, whatever the qualifications he had made, his speech would be interpreted as a passionate plea for democracy. His critics indeed had some basis for their interpretation.

After the speech there was a disagreement, one of the very last, between Palmerston and Gladstone. It was almost a confrontation of the eighteenth and nineteenth centuries. The day following the speech, Palmerston wrote: "You lay down broadly the Doctrine of Universal Suffrage which I can never accept. I entirely deny that every sane and not disqualified man has a moral right to a vote—I use that expression instead of 'the Pale of the Constitution,' because I hold that all who enjoy the security and civil rights which the Constitution provides

are within its pale—What every Man and Woman too
have a Right to, is to be well governed and under just
Laws, and they who propose a change ought to show that
the present organization does not accomplish those objects." It was the Burkean argument about the need for
representation. If there is not palpable unfairness, what
need is there for participation? But it was on these
grounds that Gladstone was arguing because he feared
that Parliament as it existed was not discharging its duties
impartially.

Also, Palmerston did not believe that opinion was maturing in the direction Gladstone maintained. "Your
Speech may win Lancashire for you, though that is doubt-
ful, but I fear it will tend to lose England for you." Gladstone retreated into a close reading of his speech, ignoring
the general impression inferred from it. He replied on
May 13: "I am at a loss to know how as you have read
my speech you can ascribe this opinion to me. . . . It
[the phrase about the pale of the Constitution] requires
I admit to be construed, but I contend that the interpretation is amply given in the speech. . . . I have never
exhorted the working men to agitate for the franchise, and
I am at a loss to conceive what report of my speech can
have been construed by you in such a sense." The correspondence went on for another week, Gladstone continuing to contend that he wanted nothing more than had
been proposed in the limited Reform Bill of 1860.[3]

The correspondence is an example of how Gladstone's
language could get him into trouble. As he wrote to a
friend of his on May 14, "I have unwarily, it seems, set
the Thames on fire. But I have great hopes that the
Thames will, on reflection perceive that he had no business or title to catch the flame, and will revert to his

ordinary temperature accordingly."[4] He did not hesitate to keep the flame burning gently. He went on a tour of Lancashire, and there he did not speak down to the multitude but treated his working-class listeners as intellectual equals.

There was a General Election in the summer of 1865, and Gladstone lost his seat as M.P. for Oxford. Even though his vestigal conservatism had led him to oppose a Bill for the elimination of religious tests for admission to the university, he was no longer conservative. Appropriately he was elected for South Lancashire, proclaiming his sense of freedom in his famous joyful remark: "At last, my friends, I am come among you, and I am come among you 'unmuzzled.' " When Palmerston died in October, Lord John Russell, who since 1861 had been in the House of Lords as Earl Russell, became Prime Minister, with Gladstone as Chancellor of the Exchequer and leader in the House of Commons. Russell was anxious to pass another Reform Bill, and a moderate one was introduced. It was opposed by the Tories, but the most intense opposition came from within the Liberal party itself, led by Robert Lowe, a devout Utilitarian, who, based on his experience of seven years in Australia and as Vice-President of the Committee of Council on Education from 1859 to 1864, maintained that those to whom it was proposed to extend the franchise were not capable of handling it. The limited extension of the franchise of 1832, combined with the weakness of the party structure since 1846, had meant that government by discussion among the upper and middle classes was something of a reality. To Lowe's mind, this was the best sort of government. It was to this contention, as well as the numerous other criticisms that had been made to Reform, that Gladstone rose to speak after 1 A.M. on the night of April 27, 1866. Specifically, the speech was made on a debate on a motion by Lord Grosvenor, a Cheshire and London magnate and the titular leader of the Lowe group. He proposed that a redistribution plan for seats be made public before a Reform Bill was passed. In its immediate object Gladstone's speech was not very successful: in the vote the Government's nominal majority fell from 70 to 5. Russell's Cabinet held on for some more tumultuous weeks, finally resigning in June.

The speech provided Gladstone with an opportunity to disclaim his own past, but at the same time to explain it rather touchingly. In the immediately previous speech, Disraeli had pointed out, with easy irony, that Gladstone had been a passionate opponent of Reform in the Oxford Union. Gladstone stated that he had "long and bitterly repented" of this belief but "I was bred under the shadow of the great name of Canning; every influence connected with that name governed the first political impressions of my childhood and my youth; with Mr. Canning I rejoiced in the removal of religious disabilities from the Roman Catholic body, and in the free and truly British tone which he gave to our policy abroad; with Mr. Canning I rejoiced in the opening he made towards the establishment of free commercial interchanges between nations; with Mr. Canning and under the shadow of that great name, and under the shadow of the yet more venerable name of Burke, I grant my youthful mind and imagination were impressed with . . . idle and futile fears." He took the opportunity presented by this attack to announce how firmly he now associated himself with the Liberals, who had "so kindly" taken him in. "I came among you an outcast from those with whom I associated, driven from them, I admit, by no arbitrary act, but by the slow and resistless forces of conviction."

Gladstone made this contrast between his earlier Tory and his present Liberal self toward the beginning of his speech, reflecting one of the few basic differences between the Liberal and the Tory approach to politics. In fact, he still tried to bridge both camps. Up until 1871 he listed himself in *Dod's,* the annual parliamentary guide, as a Liberal Conservative. Thereafter he simply called himself a Liberal. Increasingly, he seemed to share the characteristic Liberal belief that all men are potentially capable of trust, of making sensible decisions, of fending for themselves. Such a feeling helps explain both the nobility of the Liberal approach and why it was prone to overestimate the strength of the individual and abandon him to overpowering social and economic forces. The fundamental Tory attitude, which frequently could be more benevolent, was that people have to be looked after, and cannot be trusted to know their own best interests. That was the heart of the argument between Gladstone and Lowe, although Lowe placed his mistrust of the potential new voters on a more sophisticated level and in far more Utilitarian terms than did Tory country squires.

According to Gladstone, Lowe contended that the estimated 204,000 new voters admitted by the Bill would be drunken and venal, and would severely, if not irrevocably, damage the institution of Parliament. The opponents of Reform pointed out that there were already considerable numbers of working-class voters—about one quarter of the electorate—but obviously this did not impress the reformers. Gladstone's commitment to Reform deepened as the battle became more intense. He maintained that the further addition would improve Parliament, and he made his argument consistent with his constant theme of creating greater harmony among the classes. "The unreformed Parliament used to job for individuals, while the reformed Parliament jobs for classes. I do not adopt the rudeness of the phrase, but the substance of the observation is in my opinion just. . . . I believe that the composition of the House might be greatly improved; and that the increased representation of the working classes would supply us more largely with the description of Members whom we want, who would look not to the interests of classes, but to the public interest."

In an earlier interchange he had become deeply irritated with the "footling" and the haggling over figures which he found in his opponents, and in one short speech he vented his spleen on two sons of the aristocracy who were M.P.'s. To one, Lord Robert Montagu, he suggested that he might learn better manners from the workingmen he was dreading as electors, let alone fellow Members. "These working men to whom he alludes would, if admitted within these walls, set the noble Lord an example of courtesy, would set him an example of good breeding, would set him an example of high breeding, which he might do well to follow." What Gladstone found particularly unattractive about the opponents of Reform was their implication that the men who might be admitted to the franchise were at best a class enemy and at worst some sort of foreign animal that could not be tolerated within the "pale of the Constitution." He felt that too many of his opponents "were engaged in ascertaining the numbers of an invading army; but the persons to whom their remarks apply are our fellow-subjects, our fellow-Christians, our own flesh and blood, who have been lauded to the skies for their good conduct—men who have borne destitution and privation in a manner which might be a lesson to all of us." Later in the same statement he alluded to the sense of alarm that had been expressed by Lord Elcho, son of the Earl of Wemyss, about the proposed addition. "The noble Lord at the head of his Volunteers would not in the least tremble to meet a French invasion, but the idea of an invasion of his own fellow citizens desirous of obtaining the franchise has entirely frightened him from his propriety."[5]

Gladstone also made conservative arguments for Reform in the speech he delivered in its favor on April 27. There he contended that their increase in property, and their increase (harder to measure) in intelligence, virtue and loyalty, entitled a proportion of the working classes to the vote. He argued that the present state of the franchise was, in many ways, less representative than it had been before 1832. And he returned, as he had done in 1864, to the example of his new constituents, the workingmen of Lancashire, and used them as proof that Lowe was wrong in his belief that an increase in the franchise would mean the ruination of the British Constitution:

His prophecies were beautiful so far as his masterly use of the English language is concerned. But many prophecies quite as good may be found in the pages of Mr. Burke and Mr. Canning, and other almost equally distinguished men. What has been the fate of those prophecies? What use do they now serve? They form admirable material of declamations for schoolboys, and capital exercise to be translated into Greek. . . . My hon. friend says we know nothing about the labouring classes. Is not one single word a sufficient reply? The word is Lancashire. . . . The qualities then exhibited were the qualities not of select men here and there among a depraved multitude, but of the mass of a working community. . . . I cannot believe that the men who exhibited those qualities were only a sample of the people of England, and that the rest would have wholly failed in exhibiting the same great qualities had occasion arisen. I cannot see what argument could be found for some wise and temperate experiment of the extension of civil rights among such people, if the experience of the past few years does not sufficiently afford it.

Clearly, Gladstone still believed that the franchise was a privilege, not a right, but a privilege which quite a few members of the working classes had demonstrated they were fully capable of discharging with intelligence and discrimination. In fact, the Bill proposed extending the franchise to comparatively few. Gladstone ended with an emotional peroration. Despite his careful contentions throughout the speech, he could not forgo the inspirational aspects, which were making him more and more of a hero "out of doors," among the people. It was as if the Evangelical style of his childhood, buried to a degree by his new religious and political ideas, had now emerged with a new radical shape: "You cannot fight against the future. Time is on our side. The great social forces which move onwards in their might and majesty, and which the tumult of our debates does not for a moment impede or disturb—those great social forces are against you; they are marshalled on our side; and the banner which we now carry in this fight, though perhaps at some moment it may droop over our sinking heads, yet it soon again will

float in the eye of heaven, and it will be borne by the
firm hands of the united people of the three kingdoms,
perhaps not to any easy, but to a certain and to a not
distant victory."[6]

But for all his eloquence, the Bill which Gladstone was
so vehemently supporting was defeated. The Conservatives joined by discontented Liberals put an end to it,
along with the Russell ministry. Lord Derby became
Prime Minister, without a majority, and Disraeli in the
House of Commons passed, assisted by the Liberals, a
Reform Bill much more generous than the one Gladstone
had defended, admitting about one million new voters
to the franchise. Disraeli was determined to outshine
Gladstone and he had faith—ultimately justified later in
the century—in a Tory working-class vote.

Gladstone became leader of the Liberal party in December 1867, when Lord John Russell resigned. On the
Conservative side, Derby resigned as Prime Minister in
February 1868 and was replaced by Disraeli. Gladstone
and Disraeli, who were to face one another in the greatest
political battles of the nineteenth century, were now at
the top of what Disraeli referred to as the greasy pole.
In the fall of 1868 the Liberals won the General Election
with a majority of 112 seats. In December Gladstone
would be Prime Minister for the first time.

SIX

Ireland: Religion
March 1, 1869

ON DECEMBER 1, 1868, Gladstone was chopping down a tree at Hawarden when a telegram was delivered to him announcing the imminent arrival of the royal emissary to summon him to see the Queen, who would ask him to form a ministry. At that moment he turned to his companion, Evelyn Ashley, and remarked, "My mission is to pacify Ireland."

In 1845, the year of his resignation over Maynooth, he had written in a somewhat apocalyptic style to his wife: "Ireland, Ireland! that cloud in the west, that coming storm, the minister of God's retribution upon cruel and inveterate and but half-atoned injustice! Ireland forces upon us those great social and great religious questions—God grant that we may have courage to look them in the face, and to work through them."[1] In the years between he had had other matters to concern him; he was not Prime Minister, and neither his own opinions nor what he thought was the state of public opinion had matured to the extent that he thought the time proper to bring forward the question of the disestablishment of the Anglican Church in Ireland. The slowness of his change of mind as well as the gradual maturing of public opinion, made this step—which some regarded as sacrilege, blasphemy, and confiscatory—come about when it did with surprising smoothness. On this particular issue, his sense of timing, and his sense of what he must do, came together perfectly.

In 1865 he had said in Parliament that the state of the Church in Ireland was unsatisfactory, and his views on the subject had cost him his seat for Oxford. The same year he wrote to his old friend Robert Phillimore about the Church in Ireland, " *'I am not loyal to it as an Establishment.'* I could not renew the votes and speeches of thirty years back. A quarter of a century of not only fair but exceptionally fair trial has wholly dispelled hopes to which they had relation; and I am bound to say I look upon its present form of existence as no more favourable to religion, in any sense of the word, than it is to civil justice and to the contentment and loyalty of Ireland."[2]

The problem of consistency and his own religious feelings plagued him. Although he had resigned over the Maynooth grant, he had voted for it; there is no doubt that his original belief was that the role of the State was to support the true Anglican religion. He never ceased to consider that the work of God was the most important thing to be done on this earth, and that he was only useful as he was God's instrument—at times he felt that he did receive God's aid. Manning had written to him when he became Prime Minister, "And so you are at the end men live for, but not, I believe, the end for which you have lived."[3] And on February 6, 1869, *Vanity Fair* published its affectionate yet somewhat grim caricature of him with the caption "Were he a worse man, he would be a better statesman." But his ideas of how God's work was to be done had changed; he had published his book on Church and State in a flush of enthusiasm for the institution of the Church and its need to be supported by the State. He still did not believe that there should be a complete separation between Church and State; he would have fought vehemently the disestablishment of the Church of England, and after his retirement from Parliament in 1894, he even threatened to return to the fray in order to defend certain rights of the Anglican Church in Wales. He tried to maintain an uneasy middle ground. While the course of his thought was moving toward forcing religious institutions to survive without State support or protection, his emotions would not allow him to take so drastic a position. Neither emotionally nor intellectually did he ever go as far as he construed Macaulay to do in his criticism of the book on Church and State in the *Edinburgh Review:* that the State should be limited to, in its widest interpretation, police power. He never lost his belief that the State was a moral force and that its primary object was to improve those in its care. But his view on how this was to be done changed over the years.

He did feel self-conscious about now being in favor of the disestablishment of the Church of England in Ireland. In 1868 he published a pamphlet, *A Chapter of Autobiography,* in which he traced his beliefs on the subject from 1839. He rather resented the fame of *The State in Its Relations with the Church,* which he thought, with perhaps excessive modesty, had been maintained by Macaulay's review. "All interest in it [the book] had, even at that time [1841] long gone by, and it lived for nearly thirty years only in the vigorous and brilliant, though not (in my opinion) entirely faithful picture, drawn by the accomplished hand of Lord Macaulay." When the book appeared, or at least so Gladstone claimed in retrospect (even though he issued subsequent editions of it), he regarded it as a lost cause: "I found myself the last man on the sinking ship." Gladstone, so frequently held as stubborn and quixotic, was in many ways highly practical. His purpose was to do God's work, but it would be a betrayal of his trust if he did it in a way that would accomplish little or nothing. He had gone off in a noble but wrong direction and had followed his ideas more loyally than Peel or others felt he needed to when he resigned from the Cabinet in 1845. But in his own mind, he felt that in resigning he was acting properly and consistently with his earlier belief. At the same time he regarded his resignation as a propitiatory act that allowed him to move on to new views and approaches.

He felt that by voting for Maynooth he demonstrated that he no longer believed in the Anglican Church established in Ireland. His observations of religious life in England had not conformed to his expectations, but yet gave him renewed hope. He had thought originally that the Church of England would grow and encompass the religions of the Kingdoms, but he saw that instead the Church thrived if it were beleaguered. Catholics, Nonconformists, Jews, were gradually relieved of their civil disabilities. Rather than harming English society such steps enlivened and helped strengthen the Church. It emerged, he felt, in a much stronger state than the doldrums in which he had found it at Eton and Oxford. It was alive in the cities, in the colonies, in the public schools, in the universities. "The idea of asserting on her [the Church of England] part those exclusive claims, which become positively unjust in a divided country governed on popular principles, has been abandoned by all parties in the State." He still believed that there could be such a thing as a good established Church, which stood for the principle of the moral aims of the State. "Allowing for all that may be justly urged against the danger of mixing secular motives with religious administration, and above all against the intrusion of force into the domain of thought; I for one cannot desire that Constantine in the government of the empire, that Justinian in the formation of its code of laws, or that Charlemagne in refounding society, or that Elizabeth in the crisis of the English Reformation, should have acted on the principle that the State and the Church in themselves are separate or alien powers, incapable of coalition." Gladstone believed that the English establishment had adapted and had thrived on the situation in which it found itself, that there was sufficient freedom for those outside it not to challenge its particular position. But in Ireland the establishment was very much a minority church, financially supported under duress by a people of a different and antagonistic faith. In such a situation, Gladstone believed that the Church of Ireland would be helping itself to find strength and new life through disestablishment.[4]

1869 was an appropriate year for such an action. Gladstone had prepared his own mind and the minds of his supporters. The Liberals had a large majority in a House of Commons elected on a new register, and the Queen and the House of Lords were anxious not to offend the new voters. They were almost surprisingly eager to smooth the way for Gladstone to take his first steps as Prime Minister. It was under such conditions that Gladstone rose to make his three-and-a-half-hour speech introducing the Bill for the disestablishment of the Church of Ireland.

It was a speech of extraordinary command over a subject of unbelievable complexity. He had been working on plans since Christmas to deal with the sixteen million pounds worth of property held by the Church in Ireland. One of his great abilities was to put a principle in legislative form, and to do so thoroughly, and yet with economy, in every sense.

Gladstone outlined the schedule of the steps leading to disestablishment, how various vested interests, most particularly individuals supported by the Church, would be taken care of, and what would happen to the property and money of the Church. It was "the most grave and arduous work of legislation that ever has been laid before the House of Commons." Nevertheless it was absolutely necessary as "this Establishment cannot continue to exist with advantage to itself or without mischief to the country." He believed that the measure would help the cause of religion by making it far more vital in Ireland. He explained the provisions to be made for bishops, curates, glebe houses, burial grounds, and all the other vast complexities of a large religious establishment. At the same time that the State was dismantling the apparatus of a State Church, it would also withdraw what support it gave in Ireland to the Presbyterians and to Maynooth College. Even those who taught at Presbyterian educational institutions and at Maynooth would receive compensation. "With regard to them, though they are not ministers, but professors only, we propose to deal with them precisely in the same manner as if they were pastors of churches, and to assure them their salaries, together with a like power of commutation." After the various charges upon the establishment—"this great business of winding up"—were taken care of, there would be some funds left over; Gladstone felt it imperative that they be used in a noncontroversial and nonreligious way. "It is written that the money is to be applied to Irish purposes; and it is written that it is to be applied to purposes not ecclesiastical—not for any Church, not for any clergy, not for any teaching of religion . . . [yet] as nearly as circumstances admit, in conformity with what is usually the cy pres doctrine of Court of Equity," that is, that the money be used in the suitable but new way that is closest to the original intention of the donor. He recommended that the greater portion of the funds be applied to those Irish who were in difficult straits but were not so badly off that they would be helped by the Poor Law. (That law, as Gladstone admitted, "is almost intended to be niggard in its operations, because, if it were made liberal and large, the risk would then be run of doing the greatest possible injury to the independent labourer struggling to maintain himself.") The remainder of the surplus should be used to pay an Irish tax, the "country cess," which fell on all, no matter how poor, and went to assist the mad, the deaf, and the dumb, and to help provide and improve social services. With these meticulous and compassionate recommendations, he approached an end to "the almost endless arrangements" of this Act that was "great in its principles, great in the multitude of its dry, technical, but interesting detail, and great as a testing measure." As for the Church of Ireland, it would discover that like Gloucester in *King Lear* it had not fallen over any cliff at all, but would rather enter "upon a new era of existence—an era bright with hope and potent for good" after its previous existence, which was "a source of unhappiness to Ireland, and of discredit and scandal to England."[5]

He made the same points in even stronger form in a speech on the second reading of the Bill on March 23, in which he answered the various criticisms that had been made, notably an attack by Sir Stafford Northcote, once Gladstone's private secretary and now one of the leaders of the Tories. Northcote had accused the measure of being compounded of robbery and bribery. Gladstone welcomed these terms because "my right hon. friend having used those words, cannot possibly hereafter use any others that are worse, and therefore we know that we have touched the bottom." But as Gladstone chose to understand the words, they signified that the Bill would be doing its job. Robbery he took as meaning that "we have been faithful to the principles of disestablishment and general disendowment which we announced last year" and bribery that "we have studied carefully and to the best of our ability to ensure that there should be every mitigation and every softening which they [the principles] could receive in their practical application." The point of the Bill was to conciliate the Roman Catholic population of Ireland, and he argued that it was well designed for that purpose and his hearers agreed with him.[6]

The Bill passed triumphantly. It was perfectly in keeping with the aims of Gladstone's first ministry, which was dedicated to fairness, to making some attempt to eliminate those various obstacles that prevented individuals from functioning to the best of their ability. Thus, there was an Irish Land Act, which was more to be admired for its intentions than its achievements, for it did not go far enough, and was made even less efficient by the onset of the agricultural depression in 1873. Thus also, W. E.

Forster's Education Act of 1870, which laid the ground-work for free elementary education. Similarly, in 1870 the Civil Service was opened to competition by examination. An Order in Council eliminated the purchase system for military commissions as part of the modernization of the army, thereby opening up careers to talent.

Yet even this great ministry ran downhill. It had done much to open up British life and to create a Britain of probity and opportunity. If there was still exploitation and squalor, and the traditional class structure was not seriously modified, there were fewer restrictions on opportunities, and more of the talented who had not begun at the top were enabled to improve themselves and their country. As early as 1870 there were signs of difficulty, however; the House of Lords had caused trouble over the elimination of the purchase of commissions in the army, and had to be circumvented with a Royal Warrant, much to the Queen's irritation. For this and other reasons—the Queen's growing conservatism and her personal dislike of Gladstone—the relations between the Prime Minister and the Sovereign were deteriorating. Gladstone was in his prime, his parliamentary skill was at its greatest, but he displayed some of the most inevitable effects of great power: impatience with colleagues and others who hindered him in carrying out what he considered best. As politics became more tiresome, his interest in religion grew even greater, and he found himself more concerned with eternal questions rather than the immediate ones before the House of Commons. He put through valuable acts, such as the Secret Ballot Act of 1872 and the Judicature Act, which modernized the process of justice. But these were not steps with which he was particularly concerned, as he was in an attempt to establish a university in Ireland for all—which did not go far enough for Irish nationalists and Catholics, and went too far for those who supported the Protestant cause. On March 11, 1873, Gladstone was defeated by a vote of 287 to 284, with 43 Liberals (including 35 Irish) voting against him. Disraeli refused to form a minority Government, and Gladstone was forced to continue. In January 1874, Parliament was dissolved, and in the ensuing General Election Disraeli was victorious. Gladstone was temporarily exhausted of inspiring ideas: his platform centered on a proposal to eliminate the income tax. The cheeseparing side of Gladstone, though it might attract some support, was not part of his grand appeal, which rested on the use of politics for moral ends.

On January 13, 1875, he resigned from the leadership of the Liberal party. He now meant to devote himself to more lasting concerns than those of politics. "I felt myself to be in some measure," he wrote in retrospect, "out of touch with some of the tendencies of the liberal party, especially in religious matters. . . . I deeply desired an interval between parliament and the grave." He himself had done much to increase the range of Liberalism, particularly changes of approach to religious questions, and had done much to bring about the changes he now deplored. As he wrote to his wife: "I am convinced that the welfare of mankind does not now depend on the state or the world of politics; the real battle is being fought in the world of thought, where a deadly attack is being made with great tenacity of purpose and over a wide field, upon the greatest treasure of mankind, the belief in God and the gospel of Christ."[7]

The previous November he had published a pamphlet —*The Vatican Decrees in Their Bearing on Civil Al-*

legiance—attacking the doctrine of papal infallibility, which had been promulgated four years before. At the time it hadn't captured his attention—he was preoccupied with other problems, most notably the Franco-Prussian War (which broke out three days after the dogma was enunciated) —and in any case, as Prime Minister, it would have been inappropriate for him to comment. He feared it was an attempt of the Catholic Church to regain its position after the loss of its temporal powers and also as an overreaction on the part of the Roman Church to the rationalist attacks upon it. Gladstone actively sympathized with the "Old Catholics," who opposed the doctrine. The pamphlet caused a sensation, sold 145,000 copies, and brought forth twenty replies, including ones written by Manning and Newman. The essay did little to strengthen Gladstone's position with the established Anglican Church, but improved it with the "protestant conscience" of the Nonconformists, who more deeply appreciated his anti-Romanism. Certainly, it was not likely to improve his relations with the Irish Catholics. But his chief concern was to state publicly what he thought was right.

For the next two years his main interests were to remain ecclesiastical and religious. Then the "Bulgarian Atrocities" of 1876 gave him a new opportunity and impetus to combine his moral concerns with the practice of politics. The great ministry of 1868–1874 had chiefly concerned itself with domestic and Irish matters. The next segment of his career would center more on foreign affairs; on the larger stage, too, there remained his driving compulsion to attempt to achieve a greater equity in human existence, to protect or restore the rights of those who were too weak to defend themselves.

SEVEN

Foreign Policy
May 7, 1877; July 30, 1878; November 25, 1879

ONE OF GLADSTONE'S RARE ABILITIES was his capacity to be in rapport with his audience, at first in the House of Commons, and later, in addressing the vast throngs "out of doors"; in this he seemed to make up for his comparative insensitivity—his inability to recognize their moods and to allow sufficiently for their feelings—in his relations with immediate friends and colleagues. Gradually, almost reluctantly, he had become aware of his great popularity; from quite early on in his career he believed in a necessary interplay between his own ideas and what he took to be popular opinion. He first was made to recognize his appeal as a public figure during a tour of the North in 1862, particularly when he was greeted with great acclaim at Newcastle. The North of England tends to take life more seriously than the South—particularly as life there can be harder—and Gladstone's high, serious style had great appeal. And this held true even though it was on this very visit to Newcastle that he would make his unfortunate remark about Jefferson Davis creating a nation. Such a statement would go against the sentiments of most of his hearers, unless they were actually building ships for the American Confederacy.

Once he had discovered the extent of his popular support, the need for it grew upon him. But the last years of his first ministry were clouded by the belief that the masses, who had, he felt, elected him and his party in 1868, were now deserting him. He retreated into depression, illness, and disillusion, and it was almost a perverse reaction on his part that in the last six months of the ministry, when he was Chancellor of the Exchequer as well, that he emphasized his miserly qualities. He did believe that Government parsimony would help all—the poor in particular—by setting an example of thrift, but it was not an approach that commended itself, even to his most passionate supporters. His defeat in 1874 confirmed in his own mind his lack of popular support, and intensified his anxiety to turn his attention to eternal matters.

He reverted somewhat to his earlier self, the man who in 1830 wanted to go into the Church, but that was no longer, if it ever had been, his true personality. As J. L. Hammond has remarked in his study of Gladstone and Ireland, "It is difficult to think that anything but the sealed door of a a Trappist cell would have kept that impatient eager spirit out of the life of conflict in the wicked world."[1]

The issue that would bring him back into politics arose in 1876, when from April through August Turkish irregular troops—the Bashi-Bazouks—massacred twelve thousand Christian Bulgarians in suppression of a revolution. The Eastern Question yet again forced its attention upon the West. It took Gladstone some time before he decided to speak out, and considerable pressure was applied on him to do so. But when the moment was right for himself, and when he judged it was right in terms of his relations with his supporters and the country at large, he took action. The issue combined all of Gladstone's most passionate concerns—morality, the protection of Christianity, the idea of a foreign policy designed to foster a concept of nationality. For some months he continued his religious studies, his reading of Saint Thomas Aquinas, and of the Waverley novels. But then on August 31, 1876, while working on the question of future retribution in the Temple of Peace at Hawarden, he turned his mind to the question of the East. He later neatly marked on the relevant pack of papers: "From here I was called away to write on Bulgaria." But he had waited some months until he felt that the call was at the correct intensity. Then in three days he wrote the pamphlet *The Bulgarian Horrors and the Question of the East,* which was published on September 6. His anger had been intensified by what he considered the callous attitude of Disraeli, the Prime Minister, toward the massacres. As Harold Temperley has remarked, "As soon as Gladstone began to ride the whirlwind he directed the storm against the Government in general and ultimately against Disraeli in particular."[2] The pamphlet sold 40,000 copies within three or four days, and 200,000 copies in a month. Gladstone followed it up with public meetings, in which he reiterated his demand, made so powerfully in the pamphlet, that the Turks clear out of the Balkans bag and baggage (they still controlled considerable territory there). Both in the pamphlet and in his speeches, it was Gladstone at his most vehement—calculated to stir up public indignation and sympathy.

But no matter how much he came to depend on popular support, he was, above all, a dedicated parliamentarian. Always aware that policy was ultimately determined by Parliament, he stirred up outside agitation in order to force his party to support, and Parliament to take, certain steps. Gladstone wanted the government to modify its pro-Turkish policy and also to press political reforms upon the Turks.

It was a dangerous game, but Gladstone felt that morality demanded such steps. His campaign lost him to a certain extent the support of the world in which he had been born and almost completely that of the world in which he had been educated, ranging from the Queen through much of High Society. But he made up for the loss by attaching himself, at least temporarily, to the forces of popular Liberalism, the Radicals, the Nonconformists, the "Ordinary voter." He also made life rather difficult for those who led the Liberal party, notably the Marquess of Hartington, that grand Whig, who regarded himself as a Palmerstonian and felt it was less than fair that Gladstone, an allegedly retired leader, should be playing so active a role. As usual, the Gladstonian appeal was made on the basis of morality, but it was a morality firmly anchored in practical concerns. Unlike Disraeli, he recognized that the problem was not to choose between Russia and Turkey, but rather to try to find a way of enabling the Balkans to be free of both powers. Gladstone demonstrated in this controversy that he was not so much a noninterventionist in foreign affairs as a selective interventionist. But it was a position that would cause him great difficulty in his next ministry. On what basis does intervention take place, once the principle of possible intervention is accepted? Gladstone would argue the cause of morality and the best interests of Europe, but such abstractions can vary greatly depending upon who is applying them. Certainly Gladstone had a powerful point against Disraeli, who made his own task more difficult by unwisely writing that the British interests were "not affected by the question whether it was 10,000 or 20,000 persons who perished in the suppression." No matter that the thrust of the document was to condemn the severity of the Turks' reprisal. Disraeli's unfortunate phrase, as R. T. Shannon has commented, "more than any other single statement . . . made the debate on the Eastern Question from 1876 to 1880 the most clearly defined public conflict in English history on the fundamental problem of the moral nature of the State."[3]

It was a firm principle of Gladstone's that the State must not abdicate its moral role, at home or abroad. And his campaign elicited an extraordinary response. Popular political energy, previously expended on Reform, had achieved temporary satisfaction in 1867. It had not yet fastened upon Ireland, socialism, or imperialism. It could now find a great cause in the Eastern Question. The popular response to Gladstone on this issue was proof enough that between him and his followers the rapport he felt he had lost in 1874 was stronger than before. He responded to and helped shape a profound feeling of popular indignation.

He combined passion with parliamentary action. His hope was to use one to affect the other, as suggested somewhat obscurely in a letter he wrote on August 29, 1876—two days before writing his pamphlet—to Lord Granville, leader of the Liberal party in the House of Lords. He at first remarked on the electoral advantages which the Bulgarian massacres represented: "I agree that the existence of the Government should be challenged in this Election on the ground of the Bulgarian Massacres and of their conduct about them and what hangs on to them. Good ends can rarely be attained in politics without passion: and there is now, the first time for a good many years, a virtuous passion." He also noted in the same letter that Parliament had not been sufficiently consulted. His pamphlet was designed, or so it would appear, to right the balance. "I am in half, perhaps a little more than half, a mind to write a pamphlet: mainly on the ground that Parliamentary action was all but ousted. Does this shock you?"[4]

At the end of 1876 the unsuccessful Constantinople Conference was held, at which Turkish reforms were promised but not carried out. In April 1877, war began between Russia and Turkey, ending in March of 1878 with the Treaty of San Stefano. But at the Congress of Berlin, in June and July, San Stefano was undone—a triumph for Disraeli and the old diplomacy. Over a year before the Congress, Gladstone spoke against this sort of "practical" foreign policy—he had feared what might happen—although he agreed to keep the discussion vague in order not to lose support of the official leadership of his own party. At this point he reflected a great swell of popular opinion. (A little more than a year later he would take a lonelier position against the Treaty of Berlin, at a time when Beaconsfield was being received back in England with rapture and great popular enthusiasm.) It was in Parliament on May 7, 1877, that Gladstone attempted to put forward his principles in their clearest and most effective form, in a speech which Arthur Balfour, the future Tory Prime Minister, felt had never been equaled as a feat of eloquence, endurance, and skill.

In Gladstone's mind, he was still reacting to popular pressure. He wished to make that clear to the House of Commons: "The reports of nearly 100 meetings have reached me since this morning." At the same time he was speaking not just as the inadvertent head of a popular movement but as a result of his own feeling of distress about Britain's conduct. "I know of no chapter in the history of our foreign politics since the Peace of Vienna so deplorable as that of the last eighteen months." The speech became more passionate as it became increasingly a condemnation of Disraeli's policy. Disraeli supported Turkey as a counterweight to Russia and as a way of preventing Russia from moving out of the Black Sea into the Mediterranean. This was particularly important now that Disraeli had acquired for Britain a controlling interest in the Suez Canal. There, British interests were regarded as far more important than any possible moral outrage. Gladstone was sensitively aware of how easily one's humanitarian instincts were dulled; at the same time he was never fanatically against his own country; he believed that Britain's *best* interests and the cause of humanity frequently went together. In this speech he was primarily concerned with denouncing the limited and small-minded conception of British interests that had marked Disraeli's policy:

> I am sorry to say that they [the Government] seem to me to be relapsing into a position in which the outrages inflicted by the Government of Turkey are to be contemplated as matters of sentimental regret, and for idle and verbal expostulations; but in which action is to be determined by whatever we may choose to think to be British interests. That is to say, that our opinion

of what we think best for ourselves is, after all, to be, in substance, our measures of right and wrong all over the world. I want to know whether that contradiction subsists, or whether we still have to learn that there is to be no toleration for iniquity, and that no continuance of material or of moral support is to be given to a Government which is so deeply dyed with the guilt of these outrages.

Gladstone was aware that with the growth of Empire, both formal and informal, there was practically no place in which British interests were not involved, and no place where Britain could not find justification for intervention. It was thus essential that fair principles be determined by which Britain could guide herself. "Consider how from this little island we have stretched out our arms into every portion of the world. Consider how we have conquered, planted, annexed, and appropriated at all the points of the compass, so that at few points on the surface of the earth is there not some region or some spot of British dominion at hand. Nor even from these few points are we absent. Consider how our commerce finds its way into every port which a ship can enter. And then I ask you what quarrel can arise between any two countries, or what war, in which you may not, if you be so minded, set up British interests as a ground of interference." With heavy irony, Gladstone condemned the vulgar form of imperial thinking: "And then you know, Mr. Speaker, that any additions to our territory are always perfectly innocent. Sometimes they may be made not without bloodshed; sometimes they are made not without the threat of bloodshed. But that is not our fault; it is only due to the stupidity of those people who cannot perceive the wisdom of coming under our sceptre. We are endowed with a superiority of character, of noble unselfishness, an inflexible integrity which the other nations of the world are too slow to recognize; and they are stupid enough to think we—superior beings that we are —are to be bound by the same vulgar rules that might be justly applicable to the ordinary sons of Adam." What point is Gladstone making? That Britain must not consider herself morally superior to other nations, hypocritically pretending to be neither greedy nor self-seeking, at the same time that she bases every move on a calculation of how it would best serve her most immediate interests. Disraeli's policy might indeed serve Britain's immediate interest, but Gladstone maintained that it must be made subordinate to punishing the Turks for the iniquities they had inflicted upon the Balkan Christians.

Gladstone believed he had proved his point to the satisfaction of the public, if not to that of the House of Commons. "Every portion of the conduct of Turkey in regard to these massacres possesses a dramatic unity and integrity. I make bold, without asking the House to hear the repetition of the numerous details, to say that I have myself demonstrated it, in a tract now before the world, and founded on the highest evidence. Follow it out. Examine it carefully. Everything comes home to the door of the Porte [the Turkish Government] itself. . . . These massacres were not accident, they were not caprice, they were not passion. They were system, they were method, they were policy, they were principle." The moral code does not vary from domestic to foreign concerns, but must be based on the same principles: action must be taken against wrong. "You do not expostulate with malefactors in your own country—you punish them." Gladstone felt that there was little point in endless protests if there was no action intended, that in fact Turkey would be emboldened when she saw a great power continually protesting but never acting. Sarcastically he drew upon his own reputation for saving pennies. The Conservative Chancellor of the Exchequer, his former secretary Sir Stafford Northcote, generally so timorous with his old chief, had had the temerity to utter a semi-ironic Hear! Hear! when Gladstone said that one of the great problems was the attempt by the Turks to raise a huge revenue from the Christian Slav provinces. "Why should he [the Chancellor] not prepare printed forms of expostulation? There might be blanks for the number of villages burnt, for the number of men killed, and for the number of women violated; and there ought to be another blank to be filled up as occasion required by the word 'expostulate' or 'represent' or, if necessary, 'protest.' This would save a considerable amount of labour at the Foreign Office, and the Chancellor of the Exchequer, as the sovereign guardian of the public purse, might really, by the simple means that I suggest, effect some reduction in the cost of that establishment. . . . Our expostulations begin in words and . . . end in words."

In order to resolve the dilemma between British interests and moral considerations, new fair principles of international action must be sought. "I argue that we ought to use our influence in the great Council of Europe for the effectual deliverance of these Provinces from oppression, but not for their transfer to any foreign dominion." He contended that British policy was self-defeating: rather than seizing the opportunity to enable the provinces to achieve independence, Britain, by allowing the Turk to continue his oppressive ways, had forced the

Christian Slavs to look to Russia for aid. By intervening, Russia might achieve the first of Gladstone's objects, the cessation of misgovernment, but not the second, the "healthy growth of local liberty."

He felt, in effect, that Britain had sadly mismanaged the situation. He maintained that as a result of the Crimean War, Britain and her allies had forcibly taken over Russia's role as protector of the Christians under Turkish rule. "That right [of the Russians] was entirely destroyed and swept away by the Crimean War, through the expenditure of our blood and treasure, and of the blood and treasure of our Allies; and we could not thus sweep that right away, in my opinion, without becoming responsible for the consequences; without being as solemnly bound as men can be bound in faith and honour to take care that those, for whose protection it was intended, should obtain either the same thing or something better in its place." Rather than fulfilling her obligations, Britain, through continuing her support for Turkey, was helping the Turks to oppress the Christians. Britain should lead the way for the relief of the oppressed, both on her own, and with the Concert of Europe. "For my part, I think no day of peace is likely to come for the East, no final or satisfactory settlement, unless it be by the authority of united Europe." Britain must play her proper role.

So many of the traditional ruling class in Britain disagreed with him that Gladstone felt obliged to bring the power of popular opinion into diplomacy, traditionally a province reserved for the upper classes. The confrontation convinced Gladstone that those below the top level were the more reliable in their instincts of how best to behave in the world at large and in Britain itself. The result was a new intensity of feeling in the political life of London, and it would become even more marked over the question of Ireland a little less than a decade later. In his speech Gladstone denounced "the Ten Thousand," the West End of London:

> That portion of England does not express the true sentiments of England. Looking over all the great achievements that have made the last half-century illustrious, not one of them would have been effected if the opinions of the West End of London had prevailed. The Test Act would not have been repealed. Parliament would not have been reformed. Slavery would not have been abolished. Municipal Corporations would not have been opened. The Corn Laws would not have been repealed; nor Free Trade established; nor the Tariff reduced to a few lines; nor the Navigation Laws done away; nor the Universities opened; nor the Church of Ireland disestablished; nor the Land Tenures of that country re-enacted. I might extend this long list. I regard it with sorrow and misgiving that the nation has ever been in advance of those who ought to have been its leaders. But the fact being so, I cannot relax my efforts in this cause out of deference to the opinion of what I have called the West End of London.

Out of the emotion of the moment Gladstone, in a somewhat ex post facto form, had, to some extent, reconstructed the past. He made all that he considered wise in the century the consequence of the more democratic aspects of society. On the question of Bulgaria, the ruling classes had failed, he believed, while he and the "people" had coalesced on policy and principle. Like others before him, he became more democratic through disillusion with the way those in control handled a difficult situation, and also in response to what he regarded as their callousness and narrow interpretation of British interests.

Gladstone was putting forward ideals of popular and European action that contrasted, in his eyes, to the activities of the British Government. He felt that the people of Britain had found, and the Concert of Europe might also have found if the British Government had acted correctly, a moral solution to the Eastern Question. The use of force, when it was in a good cause, did not deter him. "I do not hesitate to say that the cause of the revolted subjects of Turkey against their oppressors is as holy a cause as ever animated the breast, or as ever stirred the hand of man. . . . Sir, there were other days, when England was the hope of freedom. Wherever in the world a high aspiration was entertained, or a noble blow was struck, it was to England that the eyes of the oppressed were always turned—to this favourite, this darling home of so much privilege and so much happiness, where the people that had built up a noble edifice for themselves would, it was well known, be ready to do what in them lay to secure the benefit of the same inestimable boon for others."

Gladstone felt that the true British tradition of honor and justice demanded that Britain act on behalf of the oppressed Christian Slavs. He had taken the Canningite tradition in foreign policy and expanded it through his own generous vision of what foreign policy could and should accomplish. But he would sadly rediscover during his second ministry of 1880–1885 how difficult it was to pursue an idealistic policy he approved of and at the same time placate public opinion. At this moment, however, he was able to react to, and to speak for, a considerable segment of highminded opinion, who shared with him a moral conception of policy. It was a challenging course to pursue, and one easily subject to cant and abuse, but Gladstone managed to do it, and to become the people's hero, an enemy of those "who count." Even they, as represented in the House of Commons, were stilled and impressed by this speech.[5]

Nonetheless, it was unsuccessful in its immediate object. The resolutions failed and the next week the Government majority—121—was larger than usual, even though the Liberals supported their supposedly retired leader. In fact, quite a few of them—most notably Hartington, his successor as leader in the House of Commons—had profound doubts about his policy. This was one reason Gladstone felt increasingly compelled to pursue his campaign "out of doors." He did not feel happy about the Russo-Turkish War of 1877, which had just broken out, even though he believed the Turks deserving of punishment. The Treaty of San Stefano in March 1878 ended the conflict. The great powers felt that the treaty was too favorable to Russia, and its terms were readjusted at the great Congress of Berlin the following summer. The Congress was regarded as a triumph for Bismarck and Disraeli, or rather the Earl of Beaconsfield as he now was; he had entered the House of Lords, where the strain would be less on his failing health. The Congress did not, however, solve all international problems: it left Russia dissatisfied, Turkey much reduced in her European possessions, and the Balkans as explosive as ever. But the game of the balance of power was still being played and along the lines—or so Gladstone saw them—of Beaconsfieldism, a foreign policy without morality and exclusively based, Gladstone thought, on mere calculation.

The complexity of Gladstone's conception of the role the Concert of Europe should play is revealed in his reaction to the Congress. Beaconsfield and Salisbury were the leading British negotiators. Twenty years later Salisbury acknowledged that Britain, in continuing her support of Turkey, had "backed the wrong horse." But undoubtedly in the light of British interests, the peace of Europe, and the status quo, the Congress of Berlin was a success. Beaconsfield was greeted with unbounded enthusiasm upon his return, which might have warned his rival about the changeability of public opinion.

Gladstone was becoming increasingly convinced that Disraeli was intent on misleading and corrupting the British public. That there were good aspects of the Berlin Congress made it even more imperative that the ways in which the Conservatives had failed be pointed out. In his speech on July 30, 1878, he admitted that some good had come from the treaty, most particularly in bestowing freedom upon a considerable number of Slavs. He regretted that the Slav groups dependent upon Russia had fared better than the Greeks, who had turned to Britain. But he had profound criticisms of the arrangements made and would not refrain from bringing them forward. Questions of foreign policy, dealing with national honor, created, he believed, a special need for vigilance and for speaking out: "If you forbid Members of this House to denounce, when they see cause, the policy of the Government as a dishonouring policy, I would almost go as far as to say that you may soon proceed to shut the doors of the House. By such a doctrine you will be denying to Members of Parliament what I will not now call a privilege, but what is one of their most sacred obligations." Although the results of the provisions of the

Treaty of Berlin pointed towards "the diminution of human misery, and towards the establishment of human happiness and prosperity in the East," Gladstone argued that Britain's role in the negotiations had not cast credit on what he considered the British tradition in foreign affairs. Whenever there had been a choice, Beaconsfield and Salisbury, he felt, had chosen for others servitude over freedom. They limited as far as possible the area of the new states in the Balkans, and they talked "in the tones of Metternich, and not in the tones of Mr. Canning, or of Lord Palmerston, or of Lord Russell." But these mistakes were at least within the context of a European congress; what Gladstone most profoundly objected to was the Anglo-Turkish Convention, a private agreement between the two nations that theoretically, if not practically, committed Britain to put through in Turkey an unrealistic program of reform, which she probably never hoped or intended to achieve. In return Britain received Cyprus. It was this private territorial greed that Gladstone found distasteful, and even more so that the arrangement had been made without Parliament's being given its rightful opportunity to approve or disapprove it. By this action, the Tories had violated Gladstone's European sense and had continued, as he had pointed out in his earlier speech, a pursuit of limited and selfish interests. "The whole tendency of what Her Majesty's Government has done is to establish one law for others, and another for ourselves." He maintained that the private agreement had no legal force unless the other European powers agreed to it. In effect, Gladstone charged that the British Government had acted immorally. In pursuing only her own interests and profit, she had acted beyond propriety, without the rectitude which Gladstone considered possible, although difficult, to achieve. "They [the Government] have gone beyond the limits of precedent; they have not adhered to known principles of action; they have not marched in concert with the convictions of the country, but have acted entirely without its knowledge or expectation. They have not only not developed and fulfilled the policy of former proceedings, but they have actually reversed that policy. . . . You have laid hands on the Island of Cyprus, and you will keep it as long as you please; and you have taken powers under which your sole interference with Turkey will have no limit, except such as you yourselves may choose to attach to it." And besides failing to consult Parliament, Disraeli had at once added "to the burdens which are borne with such exemplary patience by a too confiding people."[6]

In these speeches Gladstone had attempted to make clear his own conception of foreign policy. He would attempt to work in accord with it when he became Prime Minister, most particularly over the question of the British role in Egypt. There he wished to act in concert with other European powers, and also withdraw from British commitments. The situation, in Egypt and elsewhere, would work against him, however, and his attempt to reduce Britain's role would fail. His conception of foreign policy, when he was Prime Minister in his second ministry, was not put forward in speeches as important as the two just discussed on the Eastern Question. But the problem of foreign policy, especially the Eastern Question, was at the center of his famous Midlothian campaign of 1879 and in the election speeches of 1880, when he took his views to the people. He had accepted Lord Rosebery's invitation to run for a seat in Scotland held by a Tory, which would serve to intensify public interest in his campaign against "Beaconsfieldism" and the expansionist foreign policy not only in the East but in South Africa and Afghanistan, and the extravagance he held it to represent. Approximately eighty-seven thousand people heard him and his reception was tumultuous. It was an innovation to make public speeches in one's constituency when a General Election had not yet been called, and also to make whistle-stops from the train that bore him north. The two series of speeches have also been taken to mark the introduction of national political campaigns that center on the leaders of each political party.

In the first of the Midlothian speeches in Edinburgh on November 25, 1879, Gladstone presented the same concepts he had put forward in the House of Commons. He appealed to his hearers to use their good sense, and to apply it to the course which Disraeli's Government had followed. Gladstone was not a man to shirk responsibilities, nor to undervalue the strengths and capacities of his hearers. In the speech there is an almost chauvinistic paean to the strength of the people and their power within the Empire:

> Whatever is to be done in defending and governing these vast colonies with their teeming millions, in protecting that measured commerce; in relation to the enormous responsibilities of India—whatever is to be done, must be done by the force derived from you and from your children, derived from you and from your fellow-electors, throughout the land, and from you and from the citizens and people of this country. And who are they? They are, perhaps, some three-and-thirty millions of persons—a population less than the population of France; less than the population of Germany

and much less than the population of Russia. . . . We have undertaken to settle the affairs of about a fourth of the entire human race scattered over all the world. Is not that enough for the ambition of Lord Beaconsfield? . . . It is indeed deplorable that when, in addition to these calls, all manners of gratuitous, dangerous, ambiguous, impracticable, and impossible engagements are contracted for us in all parts of the world . . . I assail the policy of the Government on the highest grounds of principles. But I am now for a few moments only about to test it on the grounds of prudence. I appeal to you as practical men, I appeal to you in whatever class or profession you may be, and ask whether it is not wise to have some regard to the relation between the work to be done and the strength you possess in order to perform it.

Gladstone's view was that the commitments that Disraeli had made had gone beyond reason; that they could not and should not be fulfilled. He cited the Transvaal, Zululand, Cyprus, Egypt, the Afghan wars. And he felt that the decay was typified in the Eastern Question. Some gains had been made for humanity in the Balkans, but Britain had not fully exploited the possibilities of European concern, and had thought too much of her own limited interests. His fundamental charge was not against the expansion of British interests, although he was not happy about it, but rather over questions of method and intent. The Government had not done "right," and in this it had been supported by the majority of the House of Commons. But now at last a General Election was approaching, and the nation could declare itself. As yet, Gladstone maintained, the nation had not accepted responsibility for these actions. "If faith has been broken, if blood has been needlessly shed, if the name of England has been discredited and lowered from that lofty standard which it ought to exhibit to the whole world, if the country has been needlessly distressed, if finance has been thrown into confusion, if the foundations of the Indian Empire have been impaired, all these things as yet are the work of an Administration and a Parliament; but the day is coming, and is near at hand, when that event will take place which will lead the historian to declare whether or not they are the work, not of an Administration and not of a Parliament, but the work of a great and free people." Gladstone recognized that the electorate might choose to assume the "guilt" and "burden" of returning the Tories, but he pleaded with his listeners to work against this "resolution so full of mischief, or peril, and of shame."[7]

The tone was much more evocative and emotional than that which he used in Parliament, but the message was the same. Gladstone never asked for a simple disengagement from foreign or imperial obligations, but what he regarded as a sensible, rational, and humane limitation. He never chose the easy absolute alternatives, but rather attempted to take a middle way, fulfilling British obligations without aggrandizement. He called upon Parliament and the voters to act fairly. His position on the Eastern Question summed up the combination of moral concerns with practical politics. He wished to help the oppressed Christians in the Balkans, but within the framework of European cooperation. He respected and honored the British capacity to rule, yet he called upon his countrymen to forgo immediate interest in order to achieve the best possible solution for those who were oppressed. It was an idea that evoked a response in 1879 and again in 1880, when Gladstone made his second series of speeches in Midlothian and at whistle-stops along the way. On this grand campaign he felt that he was evoking the nation to counterbalance "the Ten Thousand." Because of his activity, but also because of economic discontent and the support of the Irish vote—as Disraeli had made the threat of Irish Home Rule his main issue of the election—the Liberals won a great victory: 347 seats against 240 Conservative M.P.'s, with 65 Irish Nationalist M.P.'s, an important independent group. The Queen hated losing Disraeli, and she hoped, as Gladstone had resigned his leadership, that Hartington or Granville would form a ministry. They knew that only Gladstone could lead; in April 1880 he formed his second ministry.

EIGHT

Religious Liberty
April 26, 1883

IN HIS SECOND MINISTRY, Gladstone attempted to cope with the imperial legacy left by Disraeli, particularly in the Transvaal and Egypt. He was reduced far more than he might have wished to a politics of reacting to other men, most particularly to the commitments Disraeli had made toward the Empire. Closer to home his politics were dominated by the Irish Question. In fact, the center of the political stage was somewhat taken away from Gladstone by the great Irish Home Rule leader, Charles Stewart Parnell. Gladstone had attempted to improve the Irish situation through land reform, although he did not feel able to abandon the policy of coercion as a way of maintaining order in Ireland. But in Gladstone's own political development one of the most significant events was his movement toward an absolute belief in the liberty of thought, as reflected in his speech on the Bradlaugh case. He had certainly traveled a long way since the days when some regarded him as a religious bigot and a prig.

Charles Bradlaugh, the well-known Victorian atheist, a believer in the abolition of the Monarchy and an advocate of birth control, President of the National Secular Society, was elected M.P. for Northampton in 1880. But when he attempted to take his oath as a Member by affirmation, his right to do so was challenged because of his lack of religious belief and hence his inability to take the oath in good conscience as it then existed. Until January 1886, he was denied membership in the House, even though his constituency continually elected him. In that month a new Speaker—the son of Sir Robert Peel— ruled that Members of the House could not challenge Bradlaugh's right to take the oath, and Lord Randolph Churchill's campaign to make political capital out of the issue came to an end. (Churchill, Arthur Balfour, John Gorst, and Henry Drummond Wolff had formed a Tory ginger group, nicknamed the Fourth party to indicate its independence and maverick nature. Its aim was to advance the careers of its members—and in the case of Churchill and Balfour it certainly succeeded—not only by taunting Gladstone and the Liberals but also the prominent figures in their own party, most notably its leader in the House of Commons, the dull Sir Stafford Northcote.)

Bradlaugh had been duly elected and reelected, but the earlier rulings and votes had maintained that he could not take the oath as an atheist nor could he "affirm," as could Quakers and others who believed in God but whose religion forbade swearing. The actions in Parliament, the role of the Irish, and the various legal and other complications are fully described in Walter Arnstein's excellent book *The Bradlaugh Case*. Here the discussion will be limited to the effect of these events upon Gladstone.

The whole protracted episode serves as a précis of the course of Gladstone's thought from the time he entered

Parliament. It reveals both the sense in which his beliefs had always been consistent (even though his remarks from the past were effectively quoted against him now) and how the nature of that consistency had changed. Gladstone reluctantly recognized that Bradlaugh was sincere and that he was a man of probity. He found Bradlaugh's beliefs, except to the degree that he was against socialism, completely distasteful, particularly his republicanism and his attacks on religion. Lord Randolph Churchill, the brilliant up-and-coming Tory leader, taunted Gladstone effectively in 1880: "Do not let it be in our power to say . . . that the first time you led the Liberal Party through the Lobby in this new Parliament was for the purpose of placing on those benches opposite an avowed Atheist and a professedly disloyal person."[1] But from the beginning Gladstone had maintained that it was exactly such cases that demanded to be treated with the utmost fairness. As he wrote to the Speaker that year, "I had no idea . . . to what extent there would be a disposition in the House to make capital out of Bradlaugh's loathsome & revolting opinions by a deviation from judicial impartiality."[2] But Gladstone was unwilling at first to take decisive action, a parallel to the slowness with which his opinions took shape throughout his life. His view on Bradlaugh's right to sit never varied, unlike his belief in the extent that he should take action on the matter. Gladstone, as always, preferred to avoid legislative innovation. And, as usual, he was the eminently practical politician: he did not wish to make Bradlaugh's right to sit a matter of a vote of confidence. He knew that his ministry might well be defeated, by a combination of dissident Liberals and the Irish M.P.'s, who either through religious conviction or policy would wish to placate Irish Catholic opinion. It would be an extremely unattractive issue upon which to go to the country. At first he did not favor a Bill that would allow Bradlaugh to affirm, and the Cabinet embarked upon putting forward such a Bill when he was away on holiday. Association with Bradlaugh was hurting the Liberals in by-elections, and petitions from the public were running strongly against Bradlaugh. But by April of 1883, Gladstone had come to believe that an Affirmation Bill was necessary, and began to prepare himself to give a speech supporting it. The Attorney-General's new young legal assistant, Herbert Asquith, prepared a "magnificent statement" for the Prime Minister on the history of oaths.[3] Gladstone delivered his speech on April 26, 1883.

To begin with, he denied that such a Bill was necessary: "I say that there is no legislative power whatever that can prevent Atheists duly elected from sitting in this House. . . . It was an accident—for it is an accident relatively to this argument—that led to the disclosure of Mr. Bradlaugh's opinions. . . . If he—whether well-advised or ill-advised is not the question—chooses to take the Oath, there is no power whatever to prevent him." Bradlaugh would have preferred to affirm, but when that choice was denied him, he considered it a greater obligation to serve his constituents than not to take the oath. Although Gladstone did not like the hypocrisy of Bradlaugh's taking the oath, he felt that the hypocrisy was forced upon him by a majority of the House. (In fact, Bradlaugh, as a true believer in his secular faith, was probably better endowed with the religious temperament than many Members of Parliament.) There had even been a considerable physical scuffle in 1881, when Bradlaugh had presented himself for the second time to Parliament; the following year he had administered the oath to himself in the Chamber. Gladstone felt that the Affirmation Bill should be passed in order to maintain the dignity of Parliament already in the process of being sorely tried by the activities in the House of the Irish Members, who were agitating for Home Rule, and by the Fourth party.

Gladstone saw the admission of Bradlaugh as a continuation of the liberalization of Britain. Catholics had been admitted to the House of Commons in 1829 and Jews in 1858. Besides, the oath had not been instituted in order to protect the established Anglican religion but rather to ensure loyalty to Queen Elizabeth when Catholics were agitating against her right to the throne. "With regard to aliens, Peers, and felons—though I am sorry to place the Peers in such company—their disqualification [to sit in Commons] rests upon the ancient and well-understood principles of the Common Law of England. The disqualification of the unbeliever rests upon nothing of the sort." Gladstone believed that an oath was between a man and his conscience; it was not the obligation of Parliament to investigate thoughts. He now fully recognized the separation of Church and State. "I know that it is said that Christianity is part of the Common Law; but am I to be told that, if it is so, every man who is not a Christian is an offender against the Common Law? If so, it is an extraordinary mode of interpreting the law."

Gladstone was profoundly aware of the problem of "guilt by association" that labeled supporters of Bradlaugh believers in atheism, republicanism, and free love. But once he saw the necessity to act, he almost welcomed the extremity of the case, as it made the obligation to be just even more imperative. And yet as a deeply religious man, he had to admit that this particular example did cause him pain. "Do you suppose that we are unaware how difficult—how all but impractical—it has become to do what we believe to be strict justice in the face of such associations? If you do not know this, you ought to know it; and if you do know, you ought not, from your place in the House, to deride us, and sarcastically to advise us to inscribe upon our banner 'Bradlaugh and Blasphemy.' Sir, I believe that every one of us intending to vote for this Bill feels that it is indeed difficult to do justice under such circumstances. But the difficulty is the measure of the duty and the honour; and just as if we were in the jury box, and a person stood before us under a criminal charge, we will put a strong hand of self-restraint upon ourselves, and we will take care that full justice—nothing more and nothing less—shall be awarded to every citizen of England."

Gladstone realized, however, that he was put in a somewhat awkward position, as he had increasingly come to believe that the "people" were more likely to be correct than "the Ten Thousand." The petitions were unquestionably running against Bradlaugh and against any Bill, like the Affirmation Bill, that would allow him to sit in Parliament. "In my opinion, upon broad questions of principle, which stand out disentangled from the surrounding facts, the immediate instincts and sense of the people are very generally right." But, considering the fine distinctions Gladstone had made in his lifetime, this situation presented no obstacle. "It does, unfortunately, sometimes happen that, when broad principles are disguised by the incidents of the case, the momentary opinion, guided by the instincts of the populace—though I do not admit that it is at all proved that it is the vast mass of the population which has petitioned in the present case —is not a safe guide." He felt that on questions of religion the populace was particularly prone to be irrational, and that political leaders must take the obligation of acting in a way that went against the immediate prejudices of many. He cited Catholic Emancipation of 1829 as an example of this necessity. (Perhaps he also used this example to chide his old friend Cardinal Manning, who had been very active in organizing Catholic and non-Catholic opinion against Bradlaugh.[4] Just the week before Gladstone's speech, Manning had been indirectly reprimanded for his actions by Cardinal Newman.)

Gladstone recognized that the Liberal party was suffering for being associated with Bradlaugh, but he felt it was for a good cause. Looking at it from a practical point of view, he was aware that eventually such causes proved to be those which the majority of the people did approve. "In every controversy that has arisen about the extension of religious toleration, and about the abatement and removal of disqualifications, in every controversy relating to religious toleration and religious disabilities, the Liberal Party has suffered before, and it is now, perhaps, suffering again; and yet it has not been a Party which, upon the whole, has had, during the last half century, the smallest or the feeblest hold upon the affections and approval of the people." In effect, he was quite justly accusing the Opposition of opportunism, and he was warning them that their immediate advantage might not last long. But advantage was secondary to principle. "There is no greater honour to a Party than to suffer in the endeavour to give effect to the principles which they believe to be just."

Gladstone was now approaching what he considered

the crux of the argument. As was typical of him through-out his career, he advanced both "conservative" and "lib-eral" arguments for his cause. After the purging effect of his resignation over Maynooth, he had come to the con-viction that the best step for the health of religion was that it should stand on its own, and not receive false support from the State. As a theocracy was not possible, religious considerations should not be a part of the dis-charge of governmental responsibility: "There is to be a total divorce between the question of religious differ-ences and the question of civil privilege and power; that there is to be no test whatever applied for a man with respect to the exercise of civil functions, except the test of civil capacity, and a fulfillment of civil conditions." This, Gladstone maintained, was the position of Lord Lyndhurst, the great Tory Lord Chancellor of the first half of the century.

But what Gladstone found particularly distressing in the opponents of Bradlaugh—and what might be called his conservative argument—was their lowering religion to the philistine level of 'I don't care what you believe, as long as you believe something,' which he expressed in his terms as "the main question for the State is not what religion a man professes, but whether he professes some religion or none." He felt that the majority of Parlia-ment, claiming to defend God, were making a mockery of religion. "They tell us that you may go any length you please in the denial of religion, provided only you do not reject the name of the Deity. They tear religion—if I may say so—in shreds, and they set aside one particular shred of it, with which nothing will ever induce them to part."

Newman and Gladstone were at one in their dislike of the kind of "religion" that was made an issue in the debate. As Newman wrote, "I cannot consider the Affirmation Bill involves a religious principle for . . . what the political and social world means by the word God is too often not the Christian nor the Jewish nor the Mahommedan God nor a personal God. . . . Hence it little concerns religion whether Mr. Bradlaugh swears by no God, or by an impersonal material, or an abstract or ideal something or other."[5]

For these reasons Gladstone came to the conclusion that a fair and absolute principle must be followed: that a legislature could not decide whether this or that constituted a true and necessary belief. He arrived at a true toleration, not from indifference but from a strong conviction of the rights of persons to believe in whatever they wished. "I am convinced that upon every religious, as well as upon every political ground, the true and wise course is not to deal with religious liberty by halves, by quarters, and by fractions; but to deal it out entire, and to leave no distinction between man and man on the ground of religious differences from one end of the land to the other." Gladstone went on to argue that the opponents of Bradlaugh who thought they were protecting the honor of Parliament, were in fact demeaning it:

A seat in this House is to the ordinary Englishman in early life, or perhaps, in middle and mature life, when he has reached a position of distinction in his career, the highest prize of his ambition. But if you place between him and that prize not only the necessity of conforming to certain civil conditions, but the adoption of certain religious words, and if these words are not justly measured to the condition of his conscience and of his convictions, you give him an inducement . . . to do violence to his conscience in order that he may not be stigmatized by being shut out from what is held to be the noblest privilege of the English citizen—that of representing his fellow-citizens in Parliament. And, therefore, I say that, besides our duty to vindicate the principle of civil and religious liberty, which totally detaches religious controversy from the enjoyment of civil rights, it is most important that the House should consider the moral effect of this test.

Gladstone suggested at the end of his speech that God was not part of these controversies, and He could look after His own interests: "We may leave the matter in His hands, and we may be quite sure that a firm and courageous application of every principle of justice and of equity is the best method we can adopt for the preservation and influence of truth." Finally, he pointed out that Parliament, by acting in such an unjust and mean way as to deny Bradlaugh his seat, was in fact helping the cause of Atheism by associating it with justice. "Unbelief attracts a sympathy which it would not otherwise enjoy; and the upshot is to impair those convictions and that religious faith, the loss of which I believe to be the most inexpressible calamity which can fall either upon a man or upon a nation."[6]

For liberty and for religion, Gladstone had pleaded that the Affirmation Bill be passed in what some considered the greatest speech he ever made. The House was profoundly stirred, but a vote was not taken then. The Bill was not voted upon until May 3, and it was then defeated by three votes: 292 to 289. It finally became law five years later, in December 1888. Gladstone's speech demonstrates the nature of his liberalism—how he was prepared to go to the outmost limits of toleration. But he held this position in the belief that such a stand was the best way to protect religion, which he no longer felt needed the State to operate in its defense. Every person should be allowed complete freedom in religion, and not be debarred by those beliefs from participation in the State. Gladstone was too devout a Christian not to move to this position with some reluctance. But he became convinced of its necessity, so that the moral state of Britain and its people could be improved.

NINE

Ireland: Home Rule
April 8, 1886

IRELAND HAD BEEN A CONTINUAL concern for Gladstone, from Maynooth on. In his thinking about Ireland he had moved in an increasingly radical direction: from disestablishment, to land laws, and now, his final great gesture, Home Rule. The taunts of foreigners who pointed to Ireland when Gladstone, the Englishman, attacked the subjugation of nationalities were not lost upon him, although from personal experience he knew Europe far better than he knew Ireland. He was there only twice, for three weeks in 1877, and for a day in Dublin in 1880. It would appear that his chief interest during his earlier trip was to hear Anglican sermons and observe how many times family prayers were said in the grand country houses he visited. That visit was made when he was in the midst of his agitation over the Eastern Question, and he could not ignore the parallels between the Balkan Slavs and the Irish Catholics. When he became Prime Minister in 1880, the pressures and his desire to respond—to find a permanent solution for Ireland—mounted. He found himself moving toward Home Rule, some form of semi-independent government for Ireland. As usual with him, it appeared as a solitary move: he kept his own counsel, yet he was responding to pressures and events. Ireland needed land reform—and he passed a highly effective Land Act in 1881, which much improved the position and independence of tenants with its assurance of fair rent, free sale, and fixity of tenure. His Government also felt it needed to pass a Coercion Act, which Gladstone heartily disliked, as a means of maintaining order in Ireland.

The Coercion Act of 1881 gave the government almost arbitrary powers of arrest. The Irish Members of Parliament, increasingly nationalistic since the Secret Ballot Act of 1872 deprived landlords of their power to press tenants to vote contrary to their wishes, had become more and more obstructive, and the procedures of the great Mother of Parliaments had to become increasingly restrictive toward debate if the Queen's Government was going to proceed. In October 1881, Parnell, although an M.P., was jailed as the progenitor of the "outrages" in Ireland, and they increased after his imprisonment. He was released in April 1882, when he agreed to support the Land Act. Tragically, Anglo-Irish relations became even more embittered the following month, when Gladstone's nephew-in-law, Lord Frederick Cavendish, the new Secretary for Ireland, was murdered in Phoenix Park in Dublin. Later Parnell would be unjustly accused of being involved in the assassination.

The Land and Coercion acts were means, neither satisfactory, of coping with Irish problems. The demands of Ireland and its Members prevented Gladstone from accomplishing much that he wished in his ministry, although it is not clear how he meant, if he had had a chance, to solve the Eastern Question. He did find himself with no choice but to occupy Egypt in 1882, following the British bombardments of Alexandria to quell a rebellion, in order to protect British control of the Suez Canal. His action was officially in defense of a joint European control of Egyptian finances—providing Germany with many opportunities to cause trouble—but to Gladstone's distress Egypt became a virtual British colony, under the rule of Lord Cromer as Consul-General.

Gladstone's Government also passed the last great Reform Act of the nineteenth century in 1884. In theory there was now complete male suffrage—at least all heads of household could vote—increasing the electorate from three to five million, or up to one in six of the population. But many remaining technical restrictions disenfranchised a considerable proportion of the population, who did not receive the vote until 1918. And no women had the vote in national elections until that year.

The difficulty in keeping a middle position in relation to the Empire was demonstrated on the occasion of the death of Gordon at the hands of the Mahdi on January 26, 1885. General Gordon had been sent by the Government to evacuate the Sudan, but he had been isolated at Khartoum, and after some hesitation and delay, Gladstone ordered a relief expedition sent to attempt to save him—it arrived two days too late. Gordon had far exceeded his orders, but most of the nation, from the Queen down, held Gladstone to blame for the death of a national hero, and gave him yet another demonstration of how fleeting a generous mood of the "people" could be. At the same time, within his own party "opinion" was getting somewhat away from his control. He had generally favored the rightist Whig wing in his Cabinet appointments—yet another manifestation of his emotional conservatism. He was not very sympathetic to Radicalism, or to Joseph Chamberlain, its most powerful proponent. Chamberlain, who had made a fortune as a screw manufacturer, had been learning to use the new voters, first through his experience as Lord Mayor of Birmingham and then in organizing the National Liberal Federation, the major support organization for the Liberal party. He was creating a new sort of popular politics that Gladstone did not find congenial.

The death of Gordon limited the days of the ministry, which was breaking up in any case over various Irish crises; it was defeated on a vote on the Budget in June 1885 by the votes of the Irish M.P.'s and Liberal abstentions. The Government resigned and the Marquess of Salisbury became Prime Minister. Disraeli's successor as leader of the party had some hope that the Tories might solve the Irish problem with some form of Home Rule—and it seemed possible, particularly as their Irish Viceroy, Lord Carnarvon, was quite sympathetic to Parnell. Gladstone liked the idea of a radical measure being passed by a Conservative Government. Such a Government could be more radical with less danger, as had happened in 1846 with the repeal of the Corn Laws and in 1867 with the passing of the second Reform Act. But it was not to work out. Salisbury, the Tory Prime Minister, called a General Election for November. The Liberals did not do too badly; they suffered in the cities because of Gordon, but they profited in the counties because of the Act of 1884 and Chamberlain's "Unauthorized Programme" of social and agrarian Reform. The Liberals had a majority of eighty-six; Parnell controlled eighty-six seats, and he had urged Irish voters in England to vote Tory. He too hoped to receive Home Rule from the Tories, and he felt it would be a smoother process because the Tories controlled the House of Lords. In December 1885 a foolish blunder by Gladstone's son Herbert, the so-called "Hawarden kite," revealed that his father was convinced of the necessity of Home Rule. The Tories, delighted to discover that they would not have to cope with a problem so unpopular with so many of their followers, were willing to see Gladstone come back in office in February, supported by the Irish.

Gladstone might have Irish support, but he was losing that of the Liberals. The Home Rule crisis alone did not split the Liberal party: those on the Whiggish side, the right of the party, had grown increasingly disaffected with the course that Gladstone was taking, his interest in democracy, his faith in the people, and his scorning of "the Ten Thousand." Even the businessmen Radicals, of whom Chamberlain would become the greatest proponent, were becoming aware that most of the goals they had wished for toward the beginning of the century had been achieved. Ireland now provided a cover as well as a genuine reason to break with the Liberal party.

As his son had accurately if prematurely reported, Gladstone was determined to attempt to pass some form of Home Rule if Salisbury did not. That was the main business of his brief third ministry from February to June 1886. Convinced that Home Rule was the just and fair solution for Ireland, he felt that the time had come to try to put it into effect. Powerful figures within the Liberal party, most notably Hartington and Joseph Chamberlain, could not agree with him, but he continued to work out his scheme, and he presented it to the House of Commons on April 8.

This was one of the last of Gladstone's great speeches, a noble and grand failure, delivered in his late seventies, when he still had twelve years to live, and one final period, still to come, as Prime Minister. He was now at the summit of his career, most elevated, and most alone. The party that he had joined in 1859, had led since 1867, was disintegrating about him: indeed, it has since been argued, despite its great victory in 1906, that in 1886 the Liberal party was mortally wounded. What Gladstone proposed, he wished to pass. He thought that the moment was politically opportune. But at the same time, he felt himself compelled to do what he believed right. This quality—of pursuing his own conception of what he must do—led him needlessly to alienate possible followers; it made him stubborn and irritable; yet it gave him grandeur and greatness.

His personality can be sensed best in the immediate preliminaries to the speech—though there had also been months of preparation. His daughter Mary has given a fine picture of the occasion. His family had always been fiercely loyal, and automatically detested whoever opposed the Grand Old Man. Thus, his wife had written to Herbert in the 1870's about hearing him speak, using "grubous," a word in the private family language, Glynnese (based on Mrs. Gladstone's maiden name: Glynne) that stood for dirty, dingy, mud-and-water-like, to describe those who were attacking her husband. "Fancy, Herbert, how grubous in the House last night, most of the beasts growling and squabbling."[1]

So now Mary described the day of the Home Rule speech in her diary:

Punch came and brought a great lump in my throat with its noble and pathetic Cartoon and poem *Sink or Swim*. . . . Excitement rather [sic] its highest pitch as we threaded [through] the waiting crowds, and I found Helen, Agnes [her sisters] and Mama all more or less quaking. . . . The rain came down in torrents, but above the storm and above the roar of London thrilled the cheers, all the way fr. D. [owning] St. we heard them, and we stared and stared as if we had never seen him before. . . . The starting of their feet of the M.P.'s, the wonderful cheers. . . . The air tingled with excitement and emotion. . . . the most quiet earnest pleading, explaining, analysing, showing a mastery of detail and a grip and grasp such as has never been surpassed. Not a sound was heard, not a cough even, only cheers breaking out here and there— a tremendous feat at his age. His voice never failed.[2]

Gladstone has left his own account of the day in his diary: "The message came to me this morning: 'Hold thou up my goings in thy path, that my footsteps slip not.' . . . Reflected much. Took a short drive. H. of C. 4½–8¼. Extraordinary scenes outside the House and in. My speech, which I have sometimes thought could never end, lasted nearly 3½ hours. Voice and strength and freedom were granted to me in a degree beyond what I could have hoped. But many a prayer had gone up for me, and not I believe in vain."[3] He felt his proposal of Home Rule to be a necessary redress of grievances.

It also led to a change in the political atmosphere in London and the comparatively easygoing nature and associations of those who ruled. The veneer cracked for a while; it was realized that over such issues as Ireland politics really mattered. John Morley, one of Gladstone's chief lieutenants on the Irish issue, remarked in the biography of his hero: "Great ladies purified their lists of the names of old intimates. Amiable magnates excluded from their dinner-tables and their country houses once familiar friends who had fallen into the guilty heresy, and even harmless portraits of the heresiarch were sternly removed from the walls. At some of the political clubs it rained blackballs."[4]

But what of the speech itself, the immediate cause of all this excitement, the summation of Gladstone's commitment to Home Rule? For the most part, considering the expectation and excitement it built up, it proved to be extremely practical as well as idealistic in its concerns. This was an appropriate tactic, for Gladstone wished to demonstrate not only the moral justice of Home Rule, but that as of a way of governing it would work efficiently and even save England money. Thus, the speech united those two essential characteristics of Gladstone: the moral man and the careful spender. He did not concern himself with the familiar problems of Ireland—land and order—which had in the past taken up so much of Parliament's time. For him, they were subsumed in the broad proposal to give Ireland partial self-government. Characteristically, he put forth as anticipated positive results that it would liberate Parliament from the restraints under which of late years it had ineffectually struggled to perform the business of the country "and restore legislation to its natural, ancient, unimpeded course." And throughout the speech he played upon the fact that the Irish business had taken so much time that it had prevented much valuable domestic legislation from coming to the fore. But his principal aim was idealistic: "the question whether it is or is not possible to establish good and harmonious relations between

Great Britain and Ireland on the footing of those free institutions to which Englishmen, Scotchmen and Irishmen are alike unalterably attached."

Granting that the number of crimes committed in Ireland had declined from the beginning of the century, he still found it lamentable that agrarian crime among the Irish had become habitual and so, too, had coercion of the Irish by the English. He wished now to break the pattern and make a fresh start, allowing the Irish to take care of their own problems. He pointed out that the Irish made particularly good soldiers of the Queen, and also were excellent in the police force, in both instances where it might be expected that they would be reluctant to submit to English control and discipline. But in these cases it was a discipline that was freely entered into; this was the secret of its success. On the other hand, there had been barely a year in which Parliament had not had to pass repressive legislation for Ireland, never truly effective because "it comes to the people of that country with a foreign aspect, and in a foreign garb." In order to achieve peace in Ireland, there must be, Gladstone felt, some sort of devolution, but without disturbing the Empire: the need was to reconcile Imperial unity with diversity of legislation. Gladstone used the example of Sweden and Norway, then united, and Austria-Hungary. (In the light of subsequent events, neither was a good choice.) Gladstone was also fully aware of the problem of Ulster. He rejected at the moment any special provision for the predominantly Protestant part of Ireland, but he felt that it was very conceivable that an acceptable plan of special provision for Ulster might emerge in the discussion of the Bill.

The practical considerations of setting up a Home government for Ireland were not overlooked. He proposed that Ireland should not continue to have representatives in Westminster. For the Parliament in Dublin he concocted a complicated scheme of two orders, one based on property, which would sit together, but could vote separately.

His Home Rule scheme was fully worked out in its financial aspects. The rich experiences Gladstone had had in the economic aspects of the State were very evident. He held it imperative that the fiscal unity of the Empire not be impaired. Certain areas would not be entrusted to the Dublin Parliament, most particularly Customs and Excise. In fact, he argued for keeping in the hands of the London Imperial Parliament the various ways in which Ireland might come in contact with the outside world. Westminster would control those areas of government that concerned the Crown, Defense, and Foreign and Colonial Relations. Also the Dublin Parliament would not be allowed to take any steps "for the establishment or the endowment of any particular religion." Certain other areas would have to be decided on the question of efficiency rather than principle, such as the Post Office. Gladstone was here divided between his belief in administrative economy and recognition of the need for local control to make devolution work. But although he left such questions open for further discussion, he displayed an acute awareness of the importance of comparatively small details in such a conception. He was not, however, immodest about the intent of the Bill: "I may be very sanguine, but I hope that the day may come when Ireland would have reason to look on this Act, if adopted by Parliament, as for practical purposes her Magna Charta. A Magna Charta for Ireland ought to be most jealously and effectively assured, and it will be assured, against unhallowed and unlawful interference."

He then discussed the economics of the relationship, how much money Ireland would receive, and how much she would have to pay for Imperial services. It was to be a contract of profit to both sides; Ireland would have more money to spend and England would have to pay far less. Gladstone regarded Home Rule as both intensely practical and idealistic: a boon that would restore, he believed, both economic and moral health to both countries. "We have sacrificed our time; we have neglected our own businesses; we have advanced our money—which I do not think at all a great favour conferred on her—and all this in the endeavour to give Ireland good laws. . . . But many of these laws have been passed under influences which can hardly be described otherwise than as influences of fear. Some of our laws have been passed in a spirit of grudging and of jealousy." Gladstone felt it might be better to be independent, and be allowed to make one's own mistakes. Keenly aware of the power of nationality, he recognized Ireland as a nation that must be allowed a certain degree of independence. His belief in the idea of nationality finally had convinced him that it applied not only to Italy, the Balkans, Greece, but just across the Irish Sea, even though he also recognized that the English Channel and the Atlantic put England and Ireland into a close relationship that must be preserved. But in many areas Ireland should rule itself, for "it is sometimes requisite not only that good laws should be passed, but also that they should be passed by the proper persons." England had come to terms with the attitude of the colonies of settlement: " 'We do not want your good laws; we want our own.' " Now she must accept the same situation in a country that had been more than a colony, but never fully integrated, except technically, into the United Kingdom. "Irish nationality vents itself in the demand for local autonomy, or separate and complete self-government in Irish, not in Imperial, affairs." Gladstone maintained that the situation between England and Ireland demanded the steps he suggested to achieve limited Home Rule. Characteristically, he also held that such steps were not only necessary, but good. "I cherish the hope that this is not merely the choice of the lesser evil, but may prove to be rather a good in itself." As he said in conclusion:

I ask the House to assist us in the work which we have undertaken, and to believe that no trivial motive can have driven us to it—to assist us in this work which, we believe, will restore Parliament to its dignity and legislation to its free and unimpeded course. I ask you to stay that waste of public treasure which is involved in the present system of government and legislation in Ireland, and which is not a waste only, but which demoralizes while it exhausts. I ask you to show to Europe and to America that we, too, can face political problems which America twenty years ago faced, and which many countries in Europe have been called upon to face, and have not feared to deal with. . . . I ask that we should apply to Ireland that happy experience which we have gained in England and in Scotland, where the course of generations has now taught us, not as a dream or a theory, but as practice and as life, that the best and surest foundation we can find to build upon is the foundation afforded by the affections, the convictions, and the will of the nation; and it is thus,

by the decree of the Almighty, that we may be enabled
to secure at once the social peace, the fame, the power,
and the permanence of the Empire.[5]

It was a noble Bill, and it was a pity that it was not
tried. Gladstone played up its economic and efficient advantages in order to try to drain away from it the emotion
that inevitably associated itself with Ireland. But the idea
of Home Rule questioned too many firmly held beliefs:
in religion, in the nature of Empire, in the menaces of
Catholicism, in the weakness of Ulster Protestantism. It
also hurt too many vested interests, most particularly
those of English landlords of Irish land. Gladstone had
wanted to put into effect what he considered the most
practical plan for coping with the Irish problem; he also
wished to demonstrate that England was a nation which
could redress grievances on a generous scale, and was capable of doing justice from a position of strength. But
Parliament would not agree, and Home Rule was delayed
until the twentieth century, when southern Irish independence came to birth in blood and civil war. On June
7, the Bill was defeated by 343 votes to 313, with 93 Liberals voting against their leader, and the Liberal Unionist
party, eventually to merge with the Tories, began to take
shape, led by Joseph Chamberlain and the Marquess of
Hartington. The Gladstone Government fell. The Marquess of Salisbury became Prime Minister; his nephew,
Arthur Balfour, a good younger family friend of the Gladstones, became a surprisingly effective Irish Secretary
from 1887 to 1891. Gladstone had hoped that his schemes
would pass; he was not the sort of politician who believed
in hopeless causes that would not work. His Home Rule

Bill and the speech presenting it, with its practicality and its idealism, reveal the unity of Gladstone's character. It was achieved through the fusing of his early religious conception of the need to serve, a compulsion to lead, with a later belief in the capacity and obligation of the people of the United Kingdom to rule themselves.

TEN

The House of Lords
March 1, 1894

HOME RULE WAS THE DOMINATING concern of the rest of Gladstone's political life. It has been said that the issue— and his preoccupation with it—rather stultified his party, but in fact his very presence, no matter what his concerns, intimidated growth. Still, he presented an extraordinary example of political dedication and prowess, with enduring power, and a belief that moral aims might be achieved through politics. That he did have faith in his own ability to continue is shown in a story he told of himself in a public speech in London in 1887:

> I met a lady, an old and esteemed friend of mine, a very kind friend, but who has the misfortune of being a strong Tory. We were talking over the recent speech of Lord Salisbury at the Carlton Club. This lady was very much annoyed that Lord Salisbury should have exhibited great fear of a dissolution. I said, "Well, it is very unreasonable indeed that he of all people in the world should dread a dissolution. Does not everybody know"—presuming to speak of myself as a symbol of

the party—"is it not an established fact that at the general election twelve months ago I was extinguished?" She said to me with considerable readiness, "Yes, but you are popping up again."

Gladstone remained the leader of the Liberal party, and did not, as he had in 1875, retire to make room for younger men; he had the cause of Ireland ever before his eyes. The voters, of whom he thought so highly, could not sustain that high pitch of altruism they had appeared to possess in 1880. The Irish cause was furthered by the dramatic clearing of Parnell's name over his alleged involvement in the assassination of Lord Frederick Cavendish in 1890 and drastically impaired later the same year through the reaction of Victorian morality to Parnell's appearing in the divorce courts when he was named as corespondent by the husband of his longtime mistress. Gladstone, more than ever dependent upon the Nonconformists, and with his own strict sense of morality (although he had known about the situation for a long time), would not support Parnell, and for this and other reasons the Irish party split. Gladstone remained loyal to Home Rule, although the Liberal party itself was changing. The National Liberal Federation at Newcastle in 1891 adopted a program that promised, besides Home Rule, disestablishment in Wales and Scotland, abolition of plural franchise, taxation of land values, triennial parliaments, district and parish councils, employers' liability, and other progressive steps, but the party lacked any coherent set of principles to tie its policies together. Gladstone, never overly sympathetic to the Radical wing or anything that partook of what he called "construction," did not, in any case, fully endorse the program.

Salisbury, in power for six years, called a General Election in 1892. Gladstone, relying on the famous swing of the pendulum, expected a comfortable majority of 100; instead he had only 40. He formed his fourth ministry, and dedicated himself to Home Rule. In September 1893, it did pass in the House of Commons, and later that month it was resoundingly defeated in the House of Lords. Gladstone's Home Rule scheme was dead, and the country did not care. Clearly his dream and hope for Home Rule were not to be his legacy to his country, and he turned to other areas, only to discover that Parliament and his Cabinet were deeply concerned about the need for increased military expenditure, contrary to his wishes. It was on this issue that he slowly allowed himself to be pushed out of office, to be succeeded as Liberal Prime Minister in March 1894 by Lord Rosebery.

He still had ideas to put forth. Indeed, he had been willing to lead the Liberal party in one last grand campaign, over the issue of the House of Lords. He was irritated that the Lords had so decisively beaten Home Rule, but he was also aware that the Lords were and would continue to be, now that Liberal peers were so rare, the great stumbling block for any significant legislation from the left. He saw the House of Lords issue as a link that would unite him with the new currents in Liberalism with which he personally had little sympathy. But his Cabinet colleagues, whatever their personal regret, thought it politically advantageous that their leader, now in his early eighties, should retire. Though in terms of the immediate situation it was probably impossible for Gladstone to continue to lead, he was still perceptive in seeing the Lords as an effective and important issue. He made that problem the subject of the last speech he gave in

Parliament as Prime Minister (although only he and the Cabinet knew that he intended to resign the office). It was also his last speech in Parliament, in any capacity, although he almost returned in June 1895 (still being an M.P.) in order to oppose his own party on several parts of the Welsh Disestablishment Bill. But the fall of the Government prevented such a characteristic pursuit of Gladstone's conception of his obligation to religion. He did emerge briefly in 1896 in order to speak in public over the Turkish massacres of Armenians. But his parliamentary life was over, sixty-one years after it had begun, with the speech he gave in the House of Commons on March 1, 1894.

The purpose of his speech was to announce that the Government, with great reluctance, would accept the amendments that the House of Lords had made to the Local Government Bill. The Lords had earlier mutilated the Employers' Liability Bill, and they were now doing the same to the Local Government Bill, which led Gladstone to reflect on the futility of the workings between the two Houses:

> The first thing that has occurred to us is this: that this operation of sending and re-sending and again resending backwards and forwards between the two houses this particular Bill is an operation which has continued long enough. I am very far, Sir, from making that observation in the interest of one House or of the other House in particular, because I confess it appears to me, and it does appear to us, that if we were to prolong this operation the result would be a considerable loss of dignity to both Houses, approaching, at a certain point, in the face of the country, almost to the ridiculous.

But he was willing to accept the Bill as amended, even though he thought that the Lords had made serious mistakes in their amendments. The particular issues were comparatively small—the Lords had ruled that there should be a population of three hundred rather than two hundred in order to have a parish council (thus trying to keep, if possible, power for the local squire), and the Lords also did not wish to transfer power over charitable trusts from the charity commissioners to the parish council, thereby showing distrust of a democratic form. But these interferences were primarily important as symptomatic of the trouble the Lords had caused throughout the session of Parliament.

> It is a mischief. In our opinion it is a gross mischief. In our opinion it is a mischief which will have to be removed upon an opportunity as early as can reasonably be found for the purpose; but, at the same time, it is a mischief limited to this portion of the objects and purposes of the Bill, and it leaves all the rest of the Bill to work freely and undisturbed. Under these circumstances, we have arrived at the conclusion that it would not be well to wreck the whole work of the Session. Except this Bill, nearly the whole work of the Session has been wrecked.

He then moved on to an even more specific denunciation of the House of Lords. He would not accept the imputation from some of the Opposition that his only interest in attacking the Lords was their defeat of his Home Rule measure, which he felt must pass eventually.

> I must observe that the sacrifice of the [Local Government] Bill forms part of a most serious question—a

question which has long been serious, which I am sorry to say, has grown more and more serious with the lapse of time, and which during the present Session has arrived at a stage of peculiar acuteness and peculiar magnitude. We look, therefore, Sir, at the question of the acceptance of these Amendments as part of a whole. We look at the acceptance of them, not as closing a controversy, except for the moment, but as handing on that prolonged controversy, which in our judgement it will be the duty of Parliament to continue until it has arrived at a satisfactory settlement. But if we were prepared to attempt to destroy what I call the whole work of the Session by consigning this Bill to the temporary oblivion to which the Irish Government Bill—[interruption, and ironical Opposition laughter]. I do not join, and I am pleased to see the large majority of those who sit opposite do not join, in the manifestation that escaped from some hon. Members. Sir, the fact is that these Amendments, and the treatment of several Bills of great importance, which this House has sent to the House of Lords after unexampled labour, raises a question of the gravest character. Two of these Bills—the Irish Government Bill and the Employers' Liability Bill—occupied this House for more than 100 days, and we meet here at the end of a Session which has doubled almost any Session upon record in the amount and intensity of its labours for the purposes of what we thought, and what the majority thought, beneficial legislation.

He felt that the situation was intolerable, and that it would soon have to be settled by the electorate, that there must be a trial of strength between the Houses. His opinion was consistent with what he had thought for a long time. He believed that the House of Commons was the supreme body in the State, although as a traditionalist he was reverent of such institutions as the Monarchy (which he had done much to bolster, despite the hatred of the Queen) and the House of Lords. He would not allow such institutions to impede forever what he and his colleagues might consider essential legislative steps. As always, he was anxious to make changes through Parliament, and bring pressure to bear there. He always recognized Parliament as the center of Government, but he was always willing to use public opinion to effect its actions. At the same time he had faith in the wisdom of the voters to make necessary changes. As he said in this speech:

The question is whether the work of the House of Lords is not merely to modify, but to annihilate the whole work of the House of Commons, work which has been performed at an amount of sacrifice—of time, of labour, of convenience, and perhaps of health—but at any rate an amount of sacrifice totally unknown to the House of Lords? Well Sir, we have not been anxious—I believe I speak for my colleagues, I know I speak my own convictions—we . . . have been desirous to save something from the wreck of the Session's work. We feel that this Bill is a Bill of such value that, upon the whole, great as we admit the objections to be to the acceptance of these Amendments, the objections are still greater and weightier to a course which would lead to the rejection of the Bill. We are compelled to accompany that acceptance with the sorrowful declaration that the differences, not of a temporary or casual nature merely, but differences of conviction, differences of prepossession, differences of mental habit, and differences of fundamental tendency, between the

House of Lords and the House of Commons, appear to
have reached a development in the present year such
as to create a state of things of which we are compelled
to say that, in our judgment, it cannot continue. Sir, I
do not wish to use hard words, which are easily employed and as easily retorted—it is a game that two can
play at—but without using hard words, without presuming to judge of motives, without desiring or ven-
turing to allege imputations, I have felt it a duty to
state what appeared to me to be indisputable facts.
The issue which is raised between a deliberative Assembly, elected by the votes of more than 6,000,000
people, and a deliberate Assembly occupied by many
men of virtue, by many men of talent, of course with
considerable diversities and varieties, is a controversy
which, when once raised, must go forward to an issue.[1]

The issue was not resolved until the Parliament Act
of 1911 virtually destroyed the power of the House of
Lords to stop legislation. Gladstone had shrewdly seen
the question as a way to bury his disagreements with his
followers by using the overreaching issue of the obstruc-
tions by the Lords. But either because they felt the time
was not right or because they were anxious to assert their
own power, the next generation of Liberal leaders would
not accept Gladstone's guidance. Not until twelve years
later—in 1906—would the Liberals again win a General
Election.

Epilogue

GLADSTONE DIED AT 4 A.M. on May 19, 1898, Ascension Day. The news of his death inspired extensive obituaries and tributes throughout the country, and indeed, throughout much of the world: a great man was gone. Perhaps the gesture that would have pleased him most occurred at the Oxford Union, which he had joined so long ago on October 22, 1829, and before whom he made his maiden speech on February 11, 1830. He had last spoken to the Union in 1890 on Homer. On his death the scheduled debate, "That the Better Half Rules the World," was adjourned in Gladstone's memory; and F. E. Smith, a Fellow of Merton College, and former President of the Union, delivered the eulogy. Smith would become the Earl of Birkenhead and one of the leading Tory politicians of the twentieth century—a distinctly modern figure. It seems fair to assume that Gladstone would have appreciated the continuity of the Union, Oxford, and politics, personified in the youthful eulogist.

He was buried in Westminster Abbey on May 28. It was an extremely grand state funeral, with a lavish attendance of official dignitaries, but it also included, which again Gladstone would have appreciated, representatives from Hawarden: thirty tenants, twelve villagers, and eighteen workmen, as well as eleven workers and the manager from the colliery that was part of the estate. Mrs. Gladstone knelt at the head of the coffin, anxious to kiss her husband one more time. She was raised by her sons, and her hand was kissed by the Prince of Wales and his eldest son, the Duke of York. The future Edward VII and George V had served as honorary pallbearers, much to Victoria's irritation. Although Gladstone had been out of power for four years, his death seemed dramatically to mark the end of an era. As the century drew to a close, so too did a way of life, a way of politics, that in many aspects had been summed up in Gladstone's own history.

Inevitably, as the reaction against the Victorian Age set in in the first thirty years of the new century, much of it was directed against Gladstone himself as one of the most eminent of Victorians. Even now, there are those who find him an unsympathetic figure. His manner is perhaps too elevated; he seems in his oratory so high flown that it may be hard to take him as seriously as he deserves, or believe that he did not contain in his makeup excessive elements of hypocrisy and priggishness. But, surely, after the shameful history of much of our century, we can feel genuine respect for a man like Gladstone, one who did not "cut his conscience" to fit the fashion of the times, an idealist who nonetheless lived out his career as a sensible and adaptable politician. Admittedly, the style of his speeches comes from a more elaborate era. Yet at their best they convey his ideas as he freshly put them forth with extraordinary command of his material, even though he generally spoke from just a few notes.

Disraeli, his great adversary, may have the advantage over Gladstone in the eyes of posterity. He was the wittier man—more detached—and more conscious of the elements of game and chance in politics. He appeals to a more cynical age. Gladstone regarded Disraeli as the great corrupter and demeaner of public life: Disraeli in return thought of Gladstone as an archvillain anxious to destroy a traditional society which Disraeli, as an outsider, valued so highly. Gladstone is continually appealing to us to be better than we are, and it is easier to escape from him by depicting him as a hypocrite, rather than to accept at face value his high seriousness and his moral earnestness. In fact, he could be a jolly companion, most particularly in family life, but that is not the picture of him drawn by his great adversary. In Disraeli's novel *Falconet,* which was never completed, the Gladstone figure is called Joseph (after Joseph Surface, the hypocrite of Sheridan's *School for Scandal*) Toplady (after the author of "Rock of Ages") Falconet. This character, according to Disraeli, had "a complete deficiency in the sense of humour. . . . His memory was vigorous, ready, and retentive; but his chief peculiarity was his disputatious temper, and the flow of language which, even as a child, was ever at command to express his arguments. . . . Joseph Toplady Falconet was essentially a prig, and among prigs there is a freemasonry which never fails. All the prigs spoke of him as the coming man."[1]

That is an easy and rather vulgar picture of Gladstone. His actions, his speeches, his career, demonstrated that he was a far more interesting man than a favorite of the prigs. If prigs are repositories of received opinions, then Gladstone would have increasingly distressed them. And he hardly had the predictable nature of a prig. There were contradictions and contrasts in his nature and in his life, which he reconciled far better than might have been expected. There were the contradictions of his mercantile background and his patrician education, although it was hardly an uncommon contrast. All through his life there was a very slight touch of the outsider about him, which made him better able to speak for and to those who were far removed from the central political world than he ever was. He could convey an extraordinary sense of sympathy and concern. His Evangelicism and his Anglo-Catholicism were contradictory religious positions, but both contributed crucial elements to his profound faith: he never ceased to regard the purpose of his life as service to God. He even attempted to contain within himself the various warring factions of the British Isles. His parents had come to England from Scotland and he maintained strong connections with their homeland; he lived much of his life as a Welsh landlord; he played out his life in English politics and sat for various English constituencies; and his last political crusade was devoted to Ireland.

He had the very qualities to appeal to the mid-Victorians. He could suggest how one could both be moral and get along in the world—an updated and comparatively sophisticated form of Protestant morality. His position was suitable for a country that was eager to play its dominant role and yearned both for power and morality. In the 1860's, Charles Francis Adams, the American Ambassador to England at the time of the Civil War, remarked of Gladstone that he was fatally weakened by the conflict between his moral convictions and his political ambitions.[2] It was the tension between these two, however, the need to resolve his private moral character with his public political ambitions, that was the very secret of his success and great strength. He was able to make his public and his private voices correspond with one another. His equation of private morality with public action helped create his great appeal to so many of his countrymen, even though some might eventually not follow him.

Gladstone's cardinal principle was that foreigners, Irish, workers, were not to be treated differently from others, and were deserving ultimately of treatment similar to that enjoyed by middle-class Englishmen. But he was not a democrat; he regarded the possibility of such treatment as a privilege, not a right. Eventually, he believed, all men (like most of his contemporaries he hardly concerned himself with the rights of women) who demonstrated their ability to do so should have power over their own affairs. Meanwhile, he was passionately opposed to despotic governments anywhere in the world. He gave to those who heard him in Britain and those who honored him abroad a sense of self-respect. He attempted to follow principles, not as abstractions in a vacuum, but as concepts that were important in everyday life; he achieved an effective correspondence of idealism and practicality. That he attempted to be honest with himself, no matter what others might think, is amply testified to by the painful pages of self-examination in his diary and his autobiographical writings. He did genuinely try to live his life according to the Sermon on the Mount, and it is amazing to what an extent he could succeed in this and still be a leader of his country during its greatest period of power. Sustained by his religion, in which his interest was "incessant, sincere, and profound," he was able to present an example of private and public character which made many feel that it was possible for politics to be both moral and effective. He was a great example; as Charles Spurgeon, the great Baptist evangelist, wrote to him in 1882: "We believe in no man's infallibility, but *it is restful to be sure of one man's integrity.*"[3]

How did he achieve his position as the dominating democrat (even though he would have rejected the term) of his day, despite all the conservative ideas and mannerisms he kept throughout his life? He himself thought that his changing attitude came from his growing love of liberty. The doctrinaire nature of his early beliefs was misleading: he had always been willing to learn. He was far more flexible than many nineteenth-century Liberals; he was not particularly influenced by the beliefs of John Locke, the philosopher of the late seventeenth century who gave special status to life and liberty—which Gladstone would have endorsed—but also to property, which Gladstone did not regard in so sacrosanct a way. Nor was he committed to the philosophy of Jeremy Bentham, the great Utilitarian, who judged all of life on principles of practicality, pain, and pleasure. He disliked both philosophies quite intensely. He had raised himself in the more generous and wide-ranging schools of Homer and Dante: his was a more romantic, compassionate, humanistic conception of human nature.

He wished to reconcile Hellenism and Christianity. (This sometimes took foolish forms, as when he attempted to demonstrate the ways in which Homer prefigured Christianity.) His efforts to do so meant that what might appear as a source of confusion resulted in an even richer conception of the wide extent of human possibilities. Homer and Dante set few limits on human achievement, did not have any set calculus. Once he came to believe that man should be free to achieve as much as he could, there were few limits set. As he said of his own life, looking back almost at its end in 1894: "It is a

career certainly chargeable with many errors of judgment, but I hope on the whole, governed at least by up-
rightness of intention and by a desire to learn. . . . It
has been predominantly a history of emancipation—that
of enabling man to do his work of emancipation, political, economical, social, moral, intellectual." The clue to
emancipation, both his own and that of his fellow countrymen and his fellow Europeans, indeed of anyone, was
liberty. "I was brought up to distrust and dislike liberty.
I learned to believe in it. That is the key to all my
changes."[4]

His position in the world as the son of a wealthy merchant and as a landlord, his education at Eton and Oxford, his own high seriousness, meant that he had a
strong concept of responsibility and service. Homer
taught him the obligation to act bravely, but a sense of
mystical Christianity contained his Hellenism. Providence could be trusted to punish if he or others made
mistakes. Paradoxically, because his religious sense
strengthened as he progressed through life he was ever
more willing to let Providence look after itself rather
than believing that it was the obligation of the State to
help it do so. He combined the sense of common exile to
be found in Dante—that every individual is in some way
on his own—with the sense of action and common country to be found in Homer.[5] It was this coming together
of unending action and striving contained within a
framework of Christian belief and a conception of the
limitations of man that enabled Gladstone to achieve for
himself a principle of order. He believed in a hierarchical society in which its members could move up step by
step, through striving and self-respect, to its highest level.
In the rapidly changing nineteenth century Gladstone,

like many another great Victorian, was looking for a principle of order that would help him understand himself and his society. Believing in hierarchy and mobility, he was able to convince himself and others that there was an idea of order in Britain from which all, and not just those who had inherited position, could profit. Christianity taught him that man has limitations and that a perfect world cannot be realized in this life. But human activity had achieved great triumphs in the nineteenth century. His own youth had been spent, to a degree, under the twin influences of the tail end of an Enlightenment belief in rationalism and the imaginative idealism of the Romantic poets. Both tended to suggest the unlimited nature of human possibility, reinforced by the more organic conception of progress subscribed to in the nineteenth century. These forces influenced Gladstone, but they were severely contained by his profound sense of Christian religion and its concepts of human limitation and sinfulness.

He did manage to convey his own ideas of dignity, self-respect, self-government, to those who followed him, either in Parliament or in the country. He had begun as the hope of the aristocracy; he ended by appealing to the mercantile interests, the Peelites, the Liberal party, the masses and the oppressed nationalities. When the themes of fairness and justice became stronger in his political ideas, many of the more sophisticated of his followers felt that he had gone too far. But he would not compromise his principles to please them, any more than he would do so to appeal to the masses. He firmly opposed the uglier sides of nationalism, as when he attacked the vulgarities of Palmerstonian saber-rattling and Disraeli on imperialism, and he had no use for jingoism.

How did Gladstone convey his hopefulness, his belief that all who heard him were capable of generous feelings and self-control, and his own goodwill and willingness to help? He was capable in his speeches of the qualities that Palmerston had noted about him, not with complete approval: enthusiasm, passion, and sympathy. It was those qualities, primarily conveyed by the spoken word, that made him such an effective orator and such a powerful politician. Without actually mirroring what the Radicals or the Nonconformists, the backbone of the Liberal party, wanted to achieve, he was able to convey both a sense of taking active steps to get to the root of the matter, which pleased the Radicals, and of serving the moral end of politics, which pleased the Nonconformists. He appeared to point a way in which the individual could realize his full capacities and be the equal of anyone. Ireland was the appropriate high point of his career; no matter that it proved a cause in which he called unsuccessfully upon his countrymen to take the just step, even if it might not be to their advantage to do so. In the case of Ireland, Gladstone demonstrated his characteristically generous spirit, which had previously been more evident in European matters. The Victorian public ultimately failed to match his generosity. But Gladstone had helped to bring that public into existence as a political force. He gave a moral dimension to the form of the State that was emerging in Britain in the course of the nineteenth century. He suggested at least the possibility that the nation might be as he wished it to be, that it might feel its way to playing a generous role in the world and favor the downtrodden.

These principles were constant; he had learned them from Peel and tried to follow them throughout his life.

As he wrote to the Queen in 1880, Peel had taught "purity in patronage, financial strictness, loyal adherence to the principle of public economy . . . strong aversion to extension of territorial responsibilities and a frank admission of the rights of foreign countries."[6] He continued to follow these principles, and added to them his own ideas of fairness and the need to assuage the feeling of class. He encased his ideas in an overwhelming sense of duty and made his principles effective through a brilliant sense of timing: seizing the right moment to act. In his parliamentary career he wished to preserve the traditional in British life, but he did not hesitate to advocate basic changes in religion, finance, political reform, foreign policy, the relations between England and Ireland, in order to suggest to the British people how they might, and indeed, how they should, live. These were his essential claims to greatness, and now, approaching a century after his death, they seem unassailable.

Source References

Prologue

1. John Morley, *The Life of Gladstone*, 2-vol. ed. (London, 1905), I, 18.
2. John Brooke and Mary Sorensen, eds., *The Prime Ministers' Papers: W. E. Gladstone*, 2 vols. (London, 1971, 1972), I, 18.
3. G. M. Young, *Mr. Gladstone* (Oxford, 1944), 10.
4. Morley, I, 70.
5. Philip Magnus, *Gladstone* (London, 1954), xi.
6. Georgina Battiscombe, *Mrs. Gladstone* (London, 1956), 82, 125, 202.
7. Information and quotations on Gladstone as landlord are from Michael Cieply, "Gladstone the Proprietor," unpublished paper, Stanford, 1975.

1. Slavery

1. Quotations are from *Hansards*, 3d ser., vol. 18, June 3, 1833, cols. 330–337.
2. M. R. D. Foot, ed., *The Gladstone Diaries*, 6 vols. (Oxford, 1968, 1975, 1978), entry for Aug. 3, 1833, I, 52.

2. Religion

1. Morley, I, 120.
2. See Alec R. Vidler, *The Orb and the Cross* (London, 1945), for a full discussion of Gladstone's early views on this subject.

3. See S. G. Checkland, *The Gladstones* (Cambridge, 1971), 253.

4. Quoted, no source given, in Magnus, 69.

5. Morley, I, 278.

6. Quotations are from *Hansards*, 3d ser., vol. 77, Feb. 4, 1845, cols. 77–82.

7. Quotations are from *Hansards*, 3d ser., vol. 115, Mar. 25, 1851, cols. 579–597.

3. Foreign Policy

1. Quotations are from A. Tilney Bassett, *Gladstone's Speeches* (London, 1916), 109–154.

2. See Marcia Pointon, "W. E. Gladstone as a Patron and Collector," *Victorian Studies* 19 (Sept. 1975) : 73–98.

3. For a detailed discussion of Gladstone and Italy, see D. M. Schreuder, "Gladstone and Italian Unification, 1848–70: The Making of a Liberal?" *English Historical Review* 85 (July 1970) : 475–501.

4. Quoted in Harold Acton, *The Last Bourbons of Naples* (London, 1961), 304.

5. Quotations are from *Hansards*, 3d ser., vol. 166, Apr. 11, 1862, cols. 933–950.

6. Quotations are from *Hansards*, 3d ser., vol. 144, Mar. 3, 1857, cols. 1787–1809.

7. Morley, I, 564.

4. Finance

1. Morley, I, 417.

2. Quoted by George Watson in *The English Ideology* (London, 1973), 127.

3. Quoted in Morley, I, 440.

4. Quotations are from Bassett, 155–181.

5. Quotations are from Bassett, 183–252.

6. Morley, I, 529.

7. Quoted in Derek Beales, *England and Italy 1859–60* (London, 1961), 87.

8. Quoted in J. B. Conacher, "Party Politics in the Age of Palmerston," *1859* (Bloomington, 1959) , 179.

9. F. E. Hyde, *Mr. Gladstone at the Board of Trade* (London, 1934) , 220.

10. Quotations are from Bassett, 253–311.

11. A remark made in 1879 (Morley, 3-vol. ed. [London, 1903], II, 63) and quoted in Richard Gunther, "Cheese-Parings and Candle-Ends: Budgeting in Gladstonian England," unpublished paper, University of California, Berkeley, n.d.

12. Figures from Gunther's paper (n. 11) .

5. Reform

1. Morley (2-vol. ed.) , I, 688.

2. Quotations are from *Hansards,* 3d ser., vol. 174, May 11, 1864, cols. 312–327.

3. The Palmerston/Gladstone letters are quoted from Philip Guedalla, ed., *Gladstone and Palmerston* (London, 1928) , 279–283.

4. Morley, I, 764.

5. Quotations are from *Hansards,* 3d ser., vol. 182, Mar. 23, 1866, cols. 872–874.

6. Quotations are from Bassett, 343–379.

6. Ireland: Religion

1. Morley, I, 383.

2. Morley, I, 776.

3. Morley, I, 889.

4. Quotations are from W. E. Gladstone, *A Chapter of Autobiography* (London, 1868) , 14, 25, 55, 59.

5. Quotations are from *Hansards,* 3d ser., vol. 194, Mar. 1, 1869, cols. 412–470.

6. Bassett, 380–400.

7. Morley, II, 108.

7. Foreign Policy

1. J. L. Hammond, *Gladstone and the Irish Nation* (London, 1964) , 142.
2. Harold Temperley, *The Bulgarians and Other Atrocities, 1875–8, in Light of Historical Criticism* (London, 1931) , 16.
3. R. T. Shannon, *Gladstone and the Bulgarian Agitation, 1876* (Edinburgh, 1963) , 23. I also owe to Mr. Shannon's superb book the idea of Gladstone's belief in "selective" intervention. See p. 11.
4. Agatha Ramm, ed., *The Political Correspondence of Mr. Gladstone and Lord Granville, 1868–86,* 2 vols. (Oxford, 1952, 1962) , I, 3.
5. This and previous quotations from the speech are from Bassett, 471–504.
6. Bassett, 505–552.
7. Bassett, 553–579.

8. Religious Liberty

1. Walter L. Arnstein, *The Bradlaugh Case* (Oxford, 1965) , 44.
2. Arnstein, 49.
3. Arnstein, 186.
4. Arnstein, 229–231.
5. Quoted in Hammond, 540.
6. Quotations are from Bassett, 581–600.

9. Ireland: Home Rule

1. Battiscombe, *Mrs. Gladstone,* 151.
2. Lucy Masterman, ed., *Mary Gladstone: Her Diaries and Letters* (London, 1930) , 385.
3. Morley, II, 550.
4. Morley, II, 561–562.
5. Bassett, 601–644.

10. The House of Lords

1. Quotations are from *Hansards,* 4th ser., vol. 21, Mar. 1, 1894, cols. 1146–1152.

Epilogue

1. Benjamin Disraeli, *Falconet* (London, 1927), 474, 490–499.
2. Martin Duberman, *Charles Francis Adams* (Boston, 1961), 332.
3. Both quotations are from Morley, II, 115, 139.
4. Morley, II, 775, 715.
5. See Hammond, 701–702.
6. Morley, I, 247.

Selected Bibliography

The amount of material available for a study of William Ewart Gladstone is prodigious. Given the particular emphasis of this study the most important resource is the thousands of columns in *Hansards*, the Parliamentary Debates, which are the best record available of Gladstone's speeches in the House of Commons. A. Tilney Bassett's *Gladstone's Speeches, Descriptive Index and Bibliography* (1916) reprints fourteen of the speeches and also lists speeches Gladstone gave in Parliament and elsewhere during the sixty-four years of his career. Innumerable collections of his speeches were also made during his lifetime—both parliamentary and outside of Parliament—the most famous being the *Midlothian Speeches, 1879,* recently reissued by the Leicester University Press with an introduction by M. R. D. Foot (1971). There are, of course, considerable manuscript resources available: the 749 volumes of papers in the British Museum, described by *Additions to the Manuscripts in the British Museum* (1953), and the family papers at the Flintshire Record Office at Hawarden, described in *The Guide to the Flintshire Record Office* (1974).

The available collections of almost every politician of the nineteenth century contain valuable letters written by Gladstone. Official government papers, including much Gladstone material, are generally to be found in the Public Record Office. The ongoing publication of the Gladstone diaries is a considerable addition to the material in print and useful for the consideration of Gladstone's life. The first six volumes, edited by M. R. D. Foot and H. C. G. Matthew, have been published, covering the years 1825–1868. The two classic biographies of Gladstone are the one commissioned by the family and written by his friend and, to a degree, disciple John Morley (1903) and the more recent one by Philip

Magnus (1954). Also worth mentioning are Francis Birrell, *Gladstone* (1933); Erick Eyck, *Gladstone* (1938); W. E. Williams, *The Rise of Gladstone to the Leadership of the Liberal Party 1859 to 1868* (1934); M. R. D. Foot and J. L. Hammond, *Gladstone and Liberalism* (1952); and E. J. Feuchtwanger, *Gladstone* (1975).

Out of the innumerable biographies and studies of Gladstone published before 1940, Howard Malchow and I recently chose those we thought especially meritorious. They are listed below. Also included are some collections of letters and some books by Gladstone himself.

Brooks, George, *Mr. Gladstone and English Politics* (1889).

Burdett, Osbert, *W. E. Gladstone* (1927).

Buxton, Sydney, *Mr. Gladstone as Chancellor of the Exchequer: A Study* (1901).

Gladstone, Herbert, *After Thirty Years* (1929).

Hamilton, Edward W., *Mr. Gladstone: A Monograph* (1898).

Hirst, Francis W., *Gladstone as Financier and Economist* (1931).

Hyde, Francis E., *Mr. Gladstone at the Board of Trade* (1934).

Lucy, Henry W., *The Right Honourable W. E. Gladstone: A Study from Life* (1895).

Paul, Herbert W., *The Life of William Ewart Gladstone* (1918).

Political Life of the Right Hon. W. E. Gladstone, The, illustrated with cartoons and sketches from *Punch*, 3 vols. (1896–1898).

Reid, Wemyss, ed., *The Life of William Ewart Gladstone* (1899).

Smith, Goldwin, *My Memory of Gladstone* (1904).

Collections of Letters

Bassett, A. Tilney, ed., *Gladstone to His Wife* (1936).

Guedalla, Philip, ed., *Gladstone and Palmerston* (1928).

———, *The Queen and Mr. Gladstone, 1845–1898*, 2 vols. (1933).

Lathbury, D. C., ed., *Correspondence on Church and Religion of William Ewart Gladstone*, 2 vols. (1910).

Masterman, Ludy, ed., *Mary Gladstone: Her Diaries and Letters* (1930).

Writings by Gladstone

Church Principles Considered in Their Results (1840).
A Chapter of Autobiography (1868).
The Vatican Decrees in Their Bearing on Civil Allegiance: A Political Expostulation (1874).
Bulgarian Horrors and the Question of the East (1876).
Gleanings of Past Years, 7 vols. (1879).
The Irish Question (1886).
Later Gleanings (1897).

Considerable material, both primary and secondary, has been published since 1940. Here I will mention only the more important books, and will exclude the many significant articles about Gladstone to be found in historical journals.

Primary Works

Brooks, John, and Mary Sorenson, eds., *The Prime Ministers' Papers: W. E. Gladstone*, 2 vols. (1971, 1972).
Hamilton, Sir Edward, *Diaries, 1880–85*, 2 vols. ed. by Dudley W. R. Bahlman (1972).
Ramm, Agatha, ed., *The Political Correspondence of Mr. Gladstone and Lord Granville, 1868–86*, 2 vols. (1952, 1962).

Books about the Gladstone Family

Battiscombe, Georgina, *Mrs. Gladstone* (1956).
Checkland, S. G., *The Gladstones: A Family Biography, 1764–1851* (1971).
Marlow, Joyce, *The Oak and the Ivy* (1977).

Almost all biographical and other secondary works on nineteenth-century British politics deal in part with Gladstone. Among the most noteworthy biographical works:

Blake, Robert, *Disraeli* (1966).
Gardiner, A. G., *The Life of Sir William Harcourt*, 2 vols. (1923).

Gash, Norman, *Mr Secretary Peel: The Life of Sir Robert Peel to 1830* (1961).

——, *Sir Robert Peel: The Life of Sir Robert Peel after 1830* (1972).

Lyons, F. S. L., *Charles Stewart Parnell* (1977).

Prest, John, *Lord John Russell* (1972).

Some Important Secondary Works

Anderson, Olive, *A Liberal State at War: English Politics and Economics During the Crimean War* (1967).

Arnstein, Walter L., *The Bradlaugh Case* (1965).

Barker, Michael K., *Gladstone and Radicalism: The Reconstruction of Liberal Policy in Britain, 1885–94* (1975).

Beales, D. E. D., *England and Italy, 1859–60* (1961).

Conacher, J. B., *The Aberdeen Coalition, 1852–55* (1968).

Cooke, A. B., and John Vincent, *The Governing Passion: Cabinet Government and Party Politics in Britain, 1885–86* (1974).

Hammond, J. L., *Gladstone and the Irish Nation* (1952).

Hanham, H. J., *Elections and Party Management: Politics in the Time of Disraeli and Gladstone* (1959).

Knaplund, P. A., *Gladstone and Britain's Imperial Policy* (1927).

——, *Gladstone's Foreign Policy* (1935).

Medlicott, W. N., *Bismarck, Gladstone and the Concert of Europe* (1956).

Newsome, David, *The Parting of Friends: A Study of the Wilberforces and Henry Manning* (1966).

O'Brien, Conor Cruise, *Parnell and His Party, 1880–90* (1957).

Schreuder, D. M., *Gladstone and Kruger: Liberal Government and Colonial "Home Rule," 1880–85* (1969).

Seton-Waton, R. W., *Disraeli, Gladstone and the Eastern Question* (1935).

Shannon, R. T., *Gladstone and the Bulgarian Agitation, 1876* (1963).

Smith, F. B., *The Making of the Second Reform Bill* (1966).

Steele, E. D., *Irish Land and British Politics* (1974).

Vidler, A. R., *The Orb and the Cross* (1945).

Vincent, John, *The Formation of the Liberal Party, 1857–1868* (1966).

Index

090925